The United States

and the

Unity of Europe

By MAX BELOFF

GREENWOOD PRESS, PUBLISHERS
WESTPORT, CONNECTICUT

Library of Congress Cataloging in Publication Data

Beloff, Max, 1913-
    The United States and the unity of Europe.

    Reprint of the ed. published by Brookings Institution,
Washington.
    Bibliography: p.
    1. Europe--Foreign relations--United States.
2. United States--Foreign relations--Europe.
3. European federation. I. Title.
[D1065.U5B4 1975]   327.73'04   75-31355
ISBN 0-8371-8507-6

Originally published in 1963 by The Brookings Institution,
Washington, D.C.

Reprinted with the permission of Brookings Institution

Reprinted in 1976 by Greenwood Press,
a division of Williamhouse-Regency Inc.

Library of Congress Catalog Card Number 75-31355

ISBN 0-8371-8507-6

Printed in the United States of America

Foreword

A UNIFIED COMMUNITY of Western states, long a dream of internationally minded reformers since the ambitious proposals of Dante and Pierre Dubois in the fourteenth century, seems at last to have some basis in reality. Compared with the abortive attempts of earlier eras, the progress made in this direction since World War II has been prodigious. The core of this development has been the concerted effort of the Six—France, Germany, Italy, Belgium, the Netherlands, and Luxembourg—to create an integrated European Community, presently based on three initial arrangements: the European Coal and Steel Community, the European Economic Community, and the European Atomic Energy Community.

While the European states have been the principal figures in this drama, the United States has played an important supplementary role. Generally, the official position of the United States government has been one of benign goodwill and support—sometimes clear and forceful, at other times clouded by uncertainty and equivocation. Currently, official policy firmly supports further strengthening of the European community. President Kennedy said in an address at Independence Hall, Philadelphia, on July 4, 1962, "We believe that a united Europe will be capable of playing a greater role in the common defense, of responding more generously to the needs of the poorer nations, of joining with the United States and others in lowering trade barriers, resolving problems of commerce and commodities and currency, and developing coordinated policies in all economic, political and diplomatic areas." Still these developments pose difficult questions for the United States, and more will arise as these efforts move forward.

Because of the critical importance of the United States relationship with the European unification movement—for America, for Europe, and for the world as a whole—the present study reviews the course of

United States policy on this subject since World War II and reflects briefly on how that course might evolve in the future. The author, Max Beloff, Gladstone Professor of Government and Public Administration at All Souls College, Oxford University, England, undertook the project while a visiting research professor at the Brookings Institution from September 1961 to January 1962, with the joint sponsorship and support of the Washington Center of Foreign Policy Research of the Johns Hopkins University. Brookings is indebted to the Ford Foundation for general support which has helped to make this study possible.

In accordance with the usual practice of the Brookings Institution, the author had the benefit of the counsel of an advisory committee composed of: William Diebold, Council on Foreign Relations, Theodore Geiger, National Planning Association, James King, Institute for Defense Analyses, Ben T. Moore, Twentieth Century Fund, Robert L. Osgood, School of Advanced International Studies, the Johns Hopkins University, and Raymond Thurston and Richard Vine, Department of State. The author and the Institution are indebted to this group for their helpful suggestions. Assistance was also rendered by many other governmental officials and private citizens too numerous to be listed.

This study was conducted under the general supervision of H. Field Haviland, Jr., Director of Foreign Policy Studies. A. Evelyn Breck edited the study and Helen Eisenhart prepared the index.

The views expressed in the publication are those of the author and do not purport to represent the views of the other staff members, officers, or trustees of the Brookings Institution.

Robert D. Calkins
President

March 1963

Author's Preface

THE MATERIAL FOR THIS STUDY was mainly collected during a visit to Washington in the fall of 1961, when I was the guest of the Brookings Institution and of the Washington Center of Foreign Policy Research attached to the School of Advanced International Studies of the Johns Hopkins University. For making this visit possible and for continuous helpfulness I am much indebted to the three scholars principally concerned—H. Field Haviland, Jr., Arnold Wolfers, and Francis O. Wilcox. I must also thank Robert D. Calkins, President of the Brookings Institution, and through him many other persons who made my work under their roof so pleasant.

Among academic colleagues who were particularly helpful I should like to thank especially Charles Kindleberger, of the Massachusetts Institute of Technology.

Much of the information was obtained in the course of interviews in Washington, New York, Ottawa, London, and Paris, with individuals who had taken part in the events described here. As most of them have been, and many of them still are, in American (or British or Canadian) government service, it would be improper to name them all, and invidious to name some without others. I should therefore wish to thank them collectively and to explain that my thanks are none the less sincere for being proffered in this anonymous fashion.

Max Beloff

All Souls College,
Oxford
November 1962

Contents

Introduction

THE POLICY WHICH THE UNITED STATES has followed toward Europe since the end of World War II has consisted of a number of different elements. The one I am concerned with in this study is the conscious, if intermittent, attempt to persuade a number of European countries of the advantages to them of a close political and economic integration—an idea to which the phrase "the United States of Europe" has sometimes been applied. My purpose has been to trace the development of this idea and the influence it has had on American policy, and also to discover the extent to which it represents a permanent tendency in American thinking that is therefore likely to have important future consequences.

I must insist on the point that this is only an essay, and that I have had to rely in large part on the public record. I have been fortunate in that the policies of the United States in this as in other questions are fully recorded in the annual volumes of the Council on Foreign Relations entitled *The United States in World Affairs* and in that many of the principal public documents are conveniently available in the series *Documents on American Foreign Relations,* formerly published by the World Peace Foundation and since 1952 by the Council on Foreign Relations. I have also made use of the two series published by the Royal Institute of International Affairs, the *Survey of International Affairs* and the *Documents on International Affairs.* For the period 1949–52 I have also made considerable use of the *Survey of United States International Finance,* published annually in those years by the International Finance Section of Princeton University.

For the understanding of what has lain behind the public record, I have mainly had to rely on a series of interviews with past and present members of the American foreign service and with other official and nonofficial persons, both American and non-American.

In view of the fact that this is an essay and not a narrative history, and in view of the necessary caution that must be attached to all oral historical evidence, when memories cannot be checked against documents of the period, I have largely refrained from inserting references. It will be understood that where the public record is concerned the source will normally be found in one or another of the series of volumes already referred to.

CHAPTER I

Policy Developments During World War II

THE FIRST THING THAT STRIKES ONE as one seeks for the origins of American policy in regard to the unity of Europe is that the idea of European integration lay quite outside the basic trend of American thinking as it had revealed itself in the wartime negotiations with the Allies. The United States in the interwar years had shown itself indifferent to, or indeed suspicious of, such schemes for European unity as were connected, for instance, with the name of Aristide Briand, seeing in them methods of excluding American economic interests for selfish European reasons. After the outbreak of World War II, a good deal of discussion of various projects for partial European union took place in London mainly between the representatives of governments in exile. British official opinion was favorable to developments of this kind, and the early British sketches for some form of postwar international organization of a world-wide character were much influenced by the idea that it could best be based on a series of regional councils, one of which would necessarily be a European one. And ideas of this kind received publicity from time to time through the speeches of Sir Winston Churchill.

The available documents do not throw a great deal of light on the evolution of official opinion in Washington on these questions, though a certain amount of public discussion took place. Within the various departments of the United States government, it is said that there was considerable interest, at least, in the possibility of some kind of regional grouping or federation in Europe; and that studies were made of a number of specific ideas on various kinds of economic integration, particularly in relation to specific activities or functions, such as

transport and electric power. Attention was also paid to relations between any such proposals and the position of Germany, both in terms
of the danger of a renewed German attempt at domination and in
the light of the possibility that closer integration might aid in keeping
Germany under some form of control. There was also some concern
lest a Europe which broke down the economic barriers between its
component parts might do so only at the price of raising them against
the rest of the world.

A number of studies of "American Interests in the War and in the
Peace" were made by groups under the auspices of the Council on Foreign Relations at the request of the State Department. The economic
and financial group produced a paper entitled "American Interests in
the Economic Unification of Europe with Respect to Trade Barriers,"
which is dated September 14, 1942. Its conclusion runs as follows:
"The United States would favor economic unification of Europe only
if steps are taken to avoid the creation of an autarkic continental economy. Positive American policy should aim at the interpenetration of
Europe's economy with that of the rest of the world, as well as a lowering of economic barriers within Europe. To be successful in this course,
the United States must work for the reduction of trade barriers against
European goods throughout the world, including the United States."

There is some reason to believe that in the late summer of 1942 a
paper favorable to European unification was prepared in the State Department, but its authors were informed that this did not correspond
to the general line of American thinking, and the matter was allowed
to drop. A special subcommittee of the Advisory Committee on Postwar Foreign Policy was set up to deal with "problems of European organization." This subcommittee met from June 1943 to March 1944,
but issued no report. The parent committee had actually been sus-
pended in July 1943, when a different form of planning organization
was created. In August 1943 a draft of a charter for a proposed United
Nations was submitted by a staff group, and this contained no provision for any form of regional organization.[1] The reason the United
States planners discarded this line of thought must be found not so
much in the prewar suspicions of European union, which had mainly
been of an economic kind, but rather in the administration's deter-

---

[1] See U.S. Department of State, *Postwar Foreign Policy Preparation, 1939–1945*,
Publication 3580 (February 1950) , pp. 146–48 and App. 23.

mination that the basis of postwar policy must rest on a firm agreement with the Soviet Union.[2] It was already clear that the government of the Soviet Union would look with deep suspicion on any European union, whether of a general or a partial kind.

When in March 1943 Count Coudenhove-Kalergi called his New York Congress of Pan-Europe, he secured a considerable degree of interest on the part of the American press. And on his initiative, a memorandum on Allied war aims, looking to some federal organization for Europe, was handed to the President by William Bullitt. But this was rejected by the President, who was convinced that the United States would have to accept the Soviet demand for a sphere of influence in Eastern Europe, and that federalist suggestions could only exacerbate relations between the two governments. Similar reasons help to explain the coldness with which the Churchill initiatives were received, and the insistence that the draft Charter for the United Nations should limit that body to universal institutions with no specific regional components.[3]

Even as early as 1943, however, Congress proved much more accessible than the administration to the idea that European union of some kind might well be an American interest. It seemed to be a method of applying to the European scene a system of government which was held to have proved its worth in the United States itself, and (by restricting the future possibilities of internecine warfare between the European states) of avoiding future American entanglements. Count Coudenhove-Kalergi's early supporters thus included some notable isolationist figures, as well as others of a more internationalist turn of mind.

In April 1944, the Legislative Reference Service of the Library of Congress produced a paper on the treatment of Germany after the war,[4] which was widely circulated among congressmen. This memorandum points out that "a number of those who are working on this

[2] Cf. Ruth B. Russell, *A History of the United Nations Charter* (Brookings Institution, 1958), pp. 102–09.

[3] See Count Richard N. Coudenhove-Kalergi, *An Idea Conquers the World* (London, 1953) and Arnold J. Zurcher, *The Struggle to Unite Europe 1940–1958* (New York University Press, 1958).

[4] Laura Puffer Morgan, *The Treatment of Germany after the War*, Library of Congress, Legislative Reference Service, Public Affairs Bulletin, No. 28A (April 1944).

problem, especially in England, see the only constructive answer in terms of some form of European federation or confederation. However loose such a confederation, it appears to offer the only basis for equality of treatment of Germany while at the same time making her subject to restrictions."

After surveying the various proposals for lesser confederations, and the Soviet objections to them, the memorandum looked at the American scene and went on:

> The American public seems to have given little attention to the idea of a European federation, its interest being concentrated on the "Union Now" of Clarence Streit in one of its two aspects—an Anglo-American union or a union of democracies. However, an idea is said to persist that a European union would not be an advantage to this country. This may arise from the fact that the immediate reaction of American correspondents in Geneva to the Briand Proposal of 1929 was that "Europe was ganging up against America," whereas the primary concern of Briand was´ rapprochement between France and Germany.

The main objections seen by the author of the memorandum were that Germany could only be held in check if other powers than its immediate continental neighbors took part. This would mean an organization ideally including not only the Soviet Union and Great Britain but also the United States. And quite apart from the position of the latter, it was already thought doubtful that Great Britain would be willing to commit itself to any binding arrangement.

While one must not make too much of a single memorandum of this kind, it does illustrate the fact that some of the enduring features and problems of America's postwar European policy were already perceptible in wartime. There is first of all the emphasis on the fact that the German problem is central for the future peace of Europe and that some kind of union may be the only method of permanently reconciling French and German interests. Secondly, there is the doubt whether the Soviet Union and Great Britain are to be regarded as possible members of a European union. Finally, as the bibliography to the memorandum shows quite clearly, up to this point there had been almost no American consideration of the European problem itself, since almost all the literature referred to is either British or the product of exiled Europeans.

Another of the studies made under the auspices of the Council on Foreign Relations, entitled "Problems of a Regional Security Organization," is dated November 28, 1944. This paper assumed that British policy was by then directed toward creating a Western European bloc as a military cover for Britain itself. It points out that such action would be taken as anti-Soviet in its orientation and also that there is the complication that Britain has treaty relations with Russia itself and that France will also want to revive them. It is held that such blocs and alliances would meet with an unfavorable reaction in the American public, and make it harder to bring the United States into the proposed world organization. The attitude of the American government looked to different methods of dealing with the German problem in the future, methods which essentially depended on direct relations with the Soviet Union. The paper, which includes a consideration of regional groupings in other parts of the world, including the Americas, in the end is against the whole idea:

> The foregoing analysis points to the conclusion that regional organization presents many dangers and few advantages to the future maintenance of security. If it is to exist, every possible effort should be made to limit it to an administrative role assuming responsibility only for carrying out decisions reached at the Security Council. To the extent that regional organization acquires a policy-determining function, it might tend, despite the precautionary provision of the Dumbarton draft, to focus attention upon the region and thus to impair the development of the central organization. Even as an administrative agency, it has few if any advantages over the ad hoc assemblage of members under the direct aegis of the central organization.

The relative indifference of the administration to regionalist ideas was to persist until the end of the war, since it was only after Potsdam that the United States began to reconsider the fundamentals of its wartime policy, and the relatively low position which Western Continental Europe had held in its scheme of priorities in the period when the United Nations Charter was finally completed.

In tracing the reversal of American policy that subsequently occurred, one must of course be fully aware of the complicated institutional background. The State Department had been forced to undergo a very rapid expansion with the multiplication of America's external responsibilities, and this was to continue. On the other hand, during the war and immediately afterwards, important aspects of policy were handled directly from the White House. The Treasury also had put forward claims to influence decisions in the field of foreign policy, and had for a time succeeded in introducing into American policy for Germany the idea that security was to be found in the virtual dismantling of the whole German economy. Even more important was the new role the professional military had secured and were to retain in the postwar period. It had been on military advice that the decisions had been taken that left Germany as a series of military zones of occupation with Berlin the seat of the proposed Four Power control well within the Soviet zone. And it was to be the military authorities in the United States Zone of Occupation, and their own conception of their responsibilities for the order and economic viability of that area, which were to affect the general American approach to the problem of devastated Europe more than any other factor. The United States government was forced to improvise its coordinating arrangements, but even with the creation in 1947 of the National Security Council it was still not possible to be certain on any particular matter where the final decision would lie. This gave, as will be seen, greater opportunities for individuals or particular groups to exercise their influence within the governmental system than would have been the case in one more tightly organized.

The general change in the American attitude toward Europe that made itself felt in the months following the defeat of Japan was mainly due to the increasing evidence of the Soviet government's unwillingness to play the part assigned to it in the American planning for the postwar world. The difficulties met by the Council of Foreign Ministers in their attempts to agree on principles for settling peace treaties with Italy and with Hitler's east European satellites, as well as friction between the Soviet Union and the Western Powers in the Middle and Far East, caused a rapid revision of the earlier view that the difficulties with the Soviet Union in Europe were largely of Britain's making and that the United States was not concerned with them. Congress on the whole reached this position more rapidly than the administration, and put considerable pressure on the administration to take a tougher line in Eastern Europe, without realizing the extent to which America's rapid demobilization had made anything of the kind almost out of the question. But the same evolution was clearly taking place in the administration itself. In December 1945 an article in *Collier's Magazine* by George Creel put President Truman on record as favoring a United States of Europe, and sympathies for at least some measure of economic union in Europe began to make themselves apparent in State Department circles as well.

Although by the end of 1946 there had been agreement on peace treaties with all former enemies other than Italy and Japan, this circumstance merely indicated an acceptance of a virtual division in Europe, with the Soviet Union installed in control of the countries bordering on itself.

The hardening of Soviet control made it more difficult for the United States to extend economic help to the whole of Europe as had been possible through the United Nations Relief and Rehabilitation Administration (UNRRA), and it began to restrict its assistance to Western Europe. With the virtual acceptance of a politically divided Europe, the prospect of maintaining Allied unity for the specific purpose of handling the German problem became more remote. The American proposal for some kind of long-term treaty to this end, first discussed in September 1945, was finally rejected by the Russians in April 1946. The political issues here were complicated by the continued divergences over reparations which led to the Americans halting further deliveries from their zone in May.

At the July meeting of the Council of Foreign Ministers, the long-term differences over German policy were clearly revealed. On the one hand the Russians attacked the Western Allies for not giving them a large enough share of reparations, for inadequate attention to German demilitarization and for their failure to break up what the Russians regarded as the economic basis of fascism. On the other hand, the Russians appealed to German opinion by denouncing the low level to which German industry was being restricted and by declaring that Germany should have freedom of trade and manufacture provided that there was a measure of inter-Allied control over industries giving a military potential—which in effect meant Russian participation in the management of the Ruhr.

This was acceptable to the Western Powers only if there were to be a genuine Four-Power control over Germany as had been the original intention. In his speech at Stuttgart on September 6, 1946, Secretary of

State Byrnes finally buried the spectre of "Morgenthauism." He argued for obliterating the zonal barriers, for allowing Germany to earn its own living and for giving Germans responsibility for running their own affairs, while making it clear that American troops would stay in Germany as long as those of any other country. This last point again amounted to a reversal in American thinking, since the wartime discussions had been predicated on the assumption that American troops would be withdrawn from Europe altogether within a relatively short time after the ending of hostilities.

Only the British were prepared at this time to agree to merge their zone with the American one, and negotiations to this end were completed by December. In the same month the Russians did go so far as to agree to begin work on a German peace treaty, but this did not prove fruitful, and one can say that from this time onward the Americans and the Russians were influenced by considerations of where German sympathies would lie in the new power struggle.

As far as the Americans were concerned, they had not reached this position without considerable heart-searching. The wariness they had shown toward suggestions that they might take over some of the world policing burdens of the British continued into peacetime and was fortified by the considerable hopes still placed in the machinery of the United Nations. When Churchill made his Fulton speech on March 5, 1946, calling for an alliance of the English-speaking peoples, it still evoked considerable criticism. But after the disagreements between Secretary of State James Byrnes and Secretary of Commerce Henry Wallace, leading to the latter's departure from the Cabinet, it could be said that majority opinion now recognized, however vaguely, that a Soviet challenge did exist and that American policy in Europe would have to take this fact into account.

While those concerned with matters of high policy were reconciling themselves to the new international scene, the officials responsible for the economic field were also being forced to look again at the assumptions on which they had hoped to be able to act in the postwar world. Between the end of the war and the spring of 1946, the Americans certainly hoped that economic relations between nations could be run without regard to political considerations and on the basis of freely convertible currencies and general nondiscrimination in trade. The special wartime measures of economic cooperation and the administrative apparatus built up to make them effective were allowed to disappear. Instead, the United States concentrated on securing support for the new multilateral institutions—the International Monetary Fund (IMF) and the World Bank—and looked forward to the conclusion of a general agreement on tariffs and trade, such as was ultimately achieved in 1948, after the still more ambitious scheme of an international trading organization failed of ratification.

It was hoped that the immediate dislocation due to the physical devastation of war and the suspension of the ordinary channels of trade could be met by emergency measures; by UNRRA, by loans from the Export-Import Bank, by measures designed to ease the termination of Lend-Lease, and in other ways. The fact that more than this would need to be done if there were to be any measure of recovery rapidly became apparent, and the first move toward more direct assistance for Europe came in the British Loan Agreement of December 5, 1945. But the arguments for this move were economic and not political. It was hoped that it would enable Britain to make the transition in its economic policy which would be needed if it were to participate fully in the international economic order toward which the Americans were working. And it was arguments of this kind that carried the loan through Congress in the middle of the summer of 1946. Apart from the direct aid that UNRRA had provided, which was handed over for winding up to the United Nations in 1946 and 1947, there had been some attempts on a regional basis to get the European economy going on a cooperative basis. A series of emergency economic organizations had been set up in the summer of 1945 to deal with special problems affecting the newly liberated countries. These were the European Coal Organization, which had grown up out of the Solid Fuel Division of SHAEF and which included representatives from Poland and Czechoslovakia as well as the Western countries; the European Central Inland Export Organization, the only one to which the Soviet Union belonged; and finally, the Emergency Economic Committee for Europe, which was confined to the Western countries and dealt with a number of specific problems, including the allocation of some particularly scarce resources. These organizations were, of course, entirely of an advisory nature.[5]

[5] See William Adams Brown, Jr. and Redvers Opie, *American Foreign Assistance* (Brookings Institution, 1953) , Chap. 4.

To some extent, however, they provided the background for the early development of American thinking on the possibility of a regional approach to the problem of European recovery. Early in 1946 W. W. Rostow, who was then the Assistant Chief of the German-Austrian Economic Division of the State Department, put forward the view that the unity of Germany would not be achieved without some measure of unity in Europe, and that this latter goal could best be approached by the economic path.

He therefore drafted a document in which he argued that the current tendency toward the formation of relatively exclusive blocs in Europe, which was the basis of Soviet, British, and French policy, was a highly dangerous one: "From the point of view of the West this is a policy frankly of despair, disruptive of every enunciated conception of U.S. political and economic foreign policy." It would, he argued, appear to involve the association of German sentiments or unity with the more aggressive of the two blocs, which would almost certainly prove to be the Eastern one, an attempt by each bloc to foster and maintain elements favorable to it within the other, and finally a tendency in each of them to develop into a military coalition. In this situation he thought that the Western Powers would be at a distinct disadvantage.

> From the outset [he argued] the United States would be confronted with very strong pressure to support economically and militarily the Western bloc. Confronted with the choice of supporting such a bloc or retiring to isolation, it is doubtful over a period of time whether popular sentiment in the United States would accept the former course, especially if the USSR were content to use means short of overt military action to secure its end. In short, it appears to be the main hope for the maintenance and extension of Western concepts and Western political power, that the structure of negotiation be elaborated to deal with an expanding range of issues, in Europe as elsewhere.

His solution was the setting up within the framework of the United Nations of a Council for Europe, with an assembly acting on a majority basis but normally dealing with technical problems through appropriate subcommittees, and with a Security Council on which not only the main continental European countries, including the Soviet Union, but also Great Britain and the United States would sit, and where, as in the United Nations, the principle of the veto would operate. These proposals were elaborated in a document which it was suggested the

Secretary of State might use as a brief in the forthcoming meeting of the Council of Foreign Ministers in Paris. This second formulation proposed the creation of two new related European organizations. The first of these would have been a Political Council for Europe, of which the Soviet Union, the United Kingdom, the United States, and France would be permanent members, with other members selected in rotation by the continental European countries. In addition to this body, which would take over the unfinished business of the existing Council of Foreign Ministers, there would be created a European Economic and Social Council, representing all the continental European countries, including the former enemy countries and the neutrals, which would be "primarily an administrative and coordinating body for a number of technical commissions with powers to receive and publish reports of these commissions." In addition, it would act as a link between these commissions and the Economic and Social Council (ECOSOC) of the United Nations.

While the document was given serious consideration at high level in the State Department, it was decided that the political presuppositions of the proposals were unlikely to be met. Secretary Byrnes, at any rate, was interested in the possibility of immediately concluding the peace treaties with the lesser enemy powers, and did not want to complicate his path at Paris by bringing in long-range problems. For this reason, his briefing for the Paris meeting did not in fact include the idea of a Council of Europe.

On the other hand, the economic proposals were put forward at a meeting in London of the Devastated Areas Sub-Commission of the Commission on Employment of ECOSOC. This move had not been formally cleared with the State Department, which, however, eventually gave it its approval. It was strongly supported by the Polish delegation to the London meeting, who saw in it a method of preventing the economic gap between Eastern and Western Europe from growing wider, and despite the original objections of the Russians and the Yugoslavs, agreement was eventually reached. The creation of an Economic Commission for Europe (ECE) was unanimously approved by the United Nations General Assembly meeting in New York in December 1946.[6]

[6] For the Economic Commission for Europe, see David Wightman, *Economic Cooperation in Europe* (London, 1956).

In its final form, the Economic Commission for Europe differed very markedly from the original American inspiration. In the first place, it included not only the continental European countries but also, on an equal footing, the Soviet Union, the United Kingdom, and the United States itself. It could thus not provide a possible framework for closer economic integration, and indeed retained, after the ending of the emergency operations, only a possible value as a forum for East-West negotiations on economic matters. It could not contribute directly to solving the economic and political problem of Germany, which was the very heart of the matter.

CHAPTER II

Approaches Toward
Unity, 1947–48

THE NEXT AND MORE IMPORTANT intervention of the United States in the affairs of Europe was, of course, the Marshall Plan. The history of this endeavor has been much studied, and the only concern here must be to see how far it was activated by the idea not merely of promoting the recovery of the European countries but of doing so within a new international or even supranational framework.

Once again, two impulses coincided. The bad winter of 1946–47 made the prospects of independent recovery in Europe more remote. It seemed unlikely in particular that Britain would be able to carry out the promise, which had been made in return for the American loan, to lift exchange controls and other forms of discrimination. At the same time, both parties in Congress were showing restiveness at any idea of continuing American financial aid. On April 2, 1947, Congressman Christian Herter introduced into the House a bill to set up a Select Committee on Foreign Aid.

On the political side, Britain's inability to continue its responsibilities in Greece and Turkey led to the enunciation on March 12, 1947 of the "Truman Doctrine," followed by proposals for aid to these two countries, eventually enacted on May 22. The Truman message declared it to be the policy of the United States to support free peoples who were resisting attempted subjugation by armed minorities or by outside pressures. This "help should be primarily through economic and financial aid" which was "essential to economic stability and orderly political processes."

It does not appear that the administration itself contemplated any further major political initiative in Europe. Its own discussion of the future of economic aid largely centered on the problem of its impact on America's economy and on the desirability of presenting further action in such a way as not to make it seem that the United States was simply taking over British responsibilities. It had to be a separate, and wholly American, initiative if the necessary popular support were to be forthcoming.

From other quarters there came, however, some indication of pressure for a more "integrationist" approach to European problems. On January 17, 1947, John Foster Dulles made a speech that was approved by Governor Thomas E. Dewey and Senator Arthur Vandenberg in which he declared that the reasons for desiring to see Germany unified economically were also valid for Europe as a whole, and that it was the business of the United States to take the lead in reconstructing Europe on federal lines. On March 22 resolutions were introduced into both Houses of Congress favoring the creation of a "United States of Europe," and these heralded a pressure which was to be fairly consistent for the next three years. Finally, there was the contribution of the publicists. On April 5 Walter Lippmann wrote: "to prevent the crisis which will otherwise engulf Europe and spread chaos throughout the world our aims will have to be very large—in Europe no less than an economic union and over here no less than the equivalent of a revival of Lend/Lease."

On April 26, 1947, Secretary of State Marshall returned from Moscow convinced that the Russians would not cooperate in any joint program for the solution of Europe's problems, and determined to hurry the creation of a policy planning staff under George Kennan, which had been discussed before Marshall's departure for Europe on March 4. Marshall now asked that the planning staff should get to work at once on basic proposals, and it met for this purpose on May 5.

At the same time, another group of people within the State Department, working under the auspices of the department's Committee on Foreign Aid, were producing another paper. This group included Charles Kindleberger, an expert on the position in Germany, H. van Buren Cleveland, and Ben T. Moore.

While these documents were being written, the idea that aid could be used to foster integration was making progress. On May 1 Walter Lippmann wrote: "From our point of view it would be refreshing innovation to make our contribution not to any separate governments but to Europe—if not to all of it at first, then at least to a very large part of it. In some such way as this the contribution, which we must inevitably make, would serve not merely to relieve suffering but as a premium and inducement to the unification of Europe."

The memorandum by Mr. Kindleberger and his colleagues was in circulation in an incomplete form fairly early in May, although it was not available in full until after General Marshall's Harvard speech on June 5, 1947 and was in its final form dated June 12.

The basis of this approach was clearly a political one. If active co-operation with the Russians were not possible, it was hoped that at least the friendly areas of Western Europe could be strengthened. American foreign policy should thus have two long-run objectives. The first of these was still to try for a degree of collaboration with the Soviet Union which could eventually permit such things as the international control and reduction of armaments. The second was "the securing of such strategic advantages," and the denial of such advantages to the Soviet Union, as would "improve our chances of winning a possible war with the Soviet Union."

In both respects the maintenance of the independence of continental Europe was vital. It must be kept pro-Western or at least neutral, and "Europe's three hundred and fifty million people must be allowed to play a positive international role by helping to blunt the sharpness of the antithesis between the United States and the Soviet Union." This approach tended to emphasize the desirability of agreement with the Soviet Union rather than the inevitability of conflict. Thus attention was paid not only to the desirable economic and political unification of Germany, but also to the rapid development of the functions and jurisdiction of the Economic Commission for Europe (ECE) "in exchange for joint, preferably United Nations, control of the Ruhr." Nevertheless, if the worst came to the worst at least the political and strategic position of the United States in Europe would have been strengthened.

In the short run, in order to harden the resistance of non-Communist Europe to Communist subversion, it was desirable to demonstrate to the Soviet leaders that the United States was both able and willing "to go ahead with a consistent and adequate recovery program for non-

Communist Europe with or without the USSR." For this objective, a purely economic program would be insufficient. "Non-Communist Europe must also be provided with positive goals to help fill the present ideological and moral vacuum." The only possible ideological content of such a program which could be envisaged was European unity.

The reaction to the Truman Doctrine had shown that Western Europe could not be attracted to an anti-Communist crusade—a point also emphasized by Walter Lippmann—and that therefore it was necessary to steer clear of a purely negative anti-Communist line. It was largely this fact that gave attractiveness to the idea of European unity.

> There appears to be no alternative equally effective for present-day Europe. The symbols of nationalism in France and Italy and in Germany are essentially bankrupt and in danger of being captured by reactionary and neo-fascist political elements which we do not wish to support. There is a possibility of developing tremendous emotional drive in Western Europe behind the supranational ideal of European unity. We cannot forget that it formed an essential part of the two most successful and dynamic recent European ideologies: German pan-European fascism and Communism itself.

Nevertheless the immediate impact of the symbol of European unity would have to be economic, not political:

> To avoid injuring sensitive feelings of nationalism, our appeal should be couched in terms of a European recovery plan which stresses the raising of European production and consumption through the economic and "functional" unification of Europe. In our propaganda and our diplomacy it will be necessary to stress (even exaggerate) the immediate economic benefits which will flow from the joint making of national economic policies and decisions.

But this program, of course, raised again the problem of choosing between a limitation of effort to Western Europe and an approach that would include the Soviet Union and the Communist dominated countries of Eastern Europe. The memorandum came out decisively in favor of the latter, partly on the economic argument that the industrial capacity of Western Europe, including Western Germany, had been largely developed to meet the needs of Eastern Europe in exchange for food, coal, and raw materials. There would be disadvantages in the possibilities offered to Soviet obstructionism by any program for the whole of Europe, but these were outweighed by its advantages.

In the framing of a program, national susceptibilities would have to be treated with care. The Germans must not be allowed to think that this was a license to their neighbors to use German resources for their own benefit without a corresponding benefit to Germany. On the other hand, the temptation must be resisted to continue along the lines of appealing more and more to German nationalism, a course on which in some respects the Soviet Union had already embarked. It had to be recognized that for the time being it was impossible to emphasize German national interests except at the cost of awakening fears in other European countries, and that Germany should only be brought into full cooperation in Europe's political and economic recovery when it had acquired a responsible political leadership that was generally acceptable.

The document's analysis of the economic requirements of a recovery plan led to the conclusion that the most appropriate agency for getting the European nations to unite in pursuit of common objectives would be the ECE. Under this body there should be some kind of investment and general programing subcommission to study proposed investment plans and projects, synchronize national investment plans and establish priorities.

The work of this subcommission would in the long run, it was argued, "be the most critical for European prosperity, for it would gradually shape the postwar development of the European economies." It was here that "the leverage of United States financial assistance would be used to influence this development by helping induce adherence to and fulfillment of the goals of the whole recovery plan." Such action would of course imply a willingness on America's part to relinquish the existing, largely bilateral, approach to financial aid. The use of aid to induce acceptance of and compliance with the plan should always be uppermost.

In such a European plan, attention would obviously have to be given to the maximizing of intra-European trade. One important aspect of this would be to cut down the tangle of exchange controls and bilateral arrangements that governed European payments and that, as is known, had been drawn to the attention of the department by the occupation authorities in the Bizone. In addition to currency convertibility, the recovery program, it was argued, should promote as a longer-term objective a Customs Union for Europe, and, as a more immediate step toward it, a general lowering of tariffs.

The memorandum, after once more arguing the case for including Eastern Europe in the scope of such a plan, returned inevitably to the problem of Germany. It pointed out the curious amalgam that United States policy toward Germany represented: on the one hand, relics of the war—demilitarization, disarmament, democratization, de-cartelization and so on; and on the other hand, the concern with German recovery as a necessary part of a recovery of the rest of Europe. "Like all United States foreign policy, policy in Germany is of necessity afflicted with the schizoid attitude toward the Soviet Union: solidarity forever if at all possible, but a well-protected flank if not."

The conclusion was "that all United States policies for German recovery should be tested not only according to their contribution to recovery in Germany and to the reduction of the United States financial burden in Germany, but also according to their contribution to European recovery and to the reduction of the United States burden in Europe generally."

This document may serve to illustrate one political line of thinking in the State Department at the time. Meanwhile, Under Secretary Acheson had also received from an interdepartmental committee a preliminary report suggesting that the aid program in different countries should be closely coordinated so as to take advantage of mutual assistance on a regional basis. And this document also placed emphasis on the necessity of reviving German production.

The general problems of aid policies were discussed by Mr. Acheson in a speech at Cleveland, Mississippi, on May 8, 1947 which although it did not attract much attention at the time was afterwards to be pointed to by President Truman in his *Memoirs* as a sort of prologue to the Marshall Plan, and which seems to have been intended to sound out the ground for another aid program.

Acheson's speech concentrated on the economic aspects of policy, and included an economic interpretation of the Truman Doctrine. It was thus designed in part to meet the criticisms of an unnecessarily bellicose tone in the new line of American policy. The key paragraph ran:

Since world demand exceeds our ability to supply, we are going to have to concentrate our emergency assistance where it will be most effective in building world political and economic stability, in promoting human freedom and democratic institutions, in fostering liberal trading policies and in strengthening the authority of the United Nations.

There was only a relatively subordinate reference to the idea of a collective European program, when Acheson said:

European recovery cannot be complete until the various parts of Europe's economy are working together in a harmonious whole. And the achievement of a coordinated European economy remains a fundamental objective of our foreign policy.

A different element was introduced into the debate by William Clayton, at that time the Under Secretary of State for Economic Affairs, a man with much experience in recent international economic negotiations, and a determined advocate of the general principles of free trade and nondiscrimination.[1] In a note written for his own guidance on March 5, 1947, he began with the idea that the reins of world leadership were fast slipping from "Britain's competent but now very weak hands" and that if these were to be picked up by the Soviet Union rather than the United States, there would almost certainly be war in the next decade or so with the odds against America. Therefore it was necessary to prevent a large-scale collapse of European regimes and their replacement by Communist ones. And this in turn would demand a major aid program involving both financial and technical and administrative assistance. In this memorandum no integrationist element is perceivable. He wrote a further memorandum in May and handed it to the Secretary of State on the 27th. This document began by asserting that the United States had underestimated the extent to which the European economy had been affected by the war and pointed to the fact that the economic crisis was now reflected in the political position. It would be "necessary for the President and Secretary of State to make a strong spiritual appeal to the American people to sacrifice a little themselves, to draw in their own belts just a little in order to save Europe from starvation and chaos (not from the Russians) and, at the same time, to preserve for ourselves and our children the glorious heritage of a free America." There should be a three-year grant to Europe, principally in the form of commodities.

[1] See E. C. Garwood, *Will Clayton: A Short Biography* (University of Texas Press, 1958).

This three-year grant to Europe [said Clayton] should be based on a European plan which the principal European nations, headed by the United Kingdom, France, and Italy, should work out. Such a plan should be based on a European economic federation on the order of the Belgium-Netherlands-Luxembourg Customs Union. Europe cannot recover from this war and again become independent if her economy continues to be divided into many small water-tight compartments as it is today.

One can therefore see that during April and May 1947 a good deal of integrationist doctrine, some of it political, some of it economic, was fed into the administration's consideration of the need of a new recovery program. In addition to the individuals already discussed, there were "many in the State Department, chiefly younger men of modest rank, who fervently believed that the European union was the only solution to the security and prosperity of the world, and persistently urged the use of American diplomacy and economic power to bring it about." [2] And these circles found much encouragement in Winston Churchill's consistent if somewhat ambiguous emphasis on the desirability of European union, as for instance in his speech in London on May 14.

The first document put forward by George Kennan's staff, and dated May 23, 1947, accepted the view that any program the United States could support would have to be a joint one agreed to by several European nations: "While it may be linked to individual national programs, such as the Monnet plan in France, it must, for psychological and political, as well as economic reasons, be an internationally agreed program." The program should be worked out by the European countries themselves but with the cooperation of the United States, which would also have to play a part in executing it in view of its role as an occupying power.

The planners were obviously exercised by the problem of the role which the Soviet Union and Eastern Europe should be given in such a plan. They assumed that the first proposal would be one for a general European plan which would be advanced in the ECE, but argued that this would have to be done in such a form "that the Russian satellite countries would either exclude themselves by unwillingness to accept

[2] Joseph M. Jones, *Fifteen Weeks* (Viking, 1955) , p. 231.

the proposed conditions, or agree to abandon the exclusive orientation of their economies." If the Russians proved able to block such a scheme in the ECE then an alternative forum would have to be found where they would not be present.

Another important point about this document is that it does not regard the British position as on all fours with that of the continental European countries (a subject on which there had been much debate among the Planning Staff) : "The overall European program must embrace, or be linked to, some sort of plan for dealing with the economic plight of Britain. The plan must be formally a British one, worked out on British initiative and responsibility, and the role of the United States, again, must be to give friendly support." In the light of this it is understandable that the planners thought that the general question should be examined first of all informally and secretly with the British leaders. There is reason to believe that the staff also proposed a tripartite United Kingdom—Canada—United States—currency arrangement to deal with the difficulties of sterling. But this was not proceeded with further.

It was now that Marshall came to his final conclusion about the Russians, apparently at a meeting on May 28. He then decided that the risk of not trying to bring the Russians in was too great. It was thought better, also, that no other government should have prior knowledge of the plan, and it was arranged that its first presentation should be in a speech by Marshall at Harvard on June 5, 1947.[3]

The Marshall speech was in effect a combination of the memoranda by Clayton on the one hand and by Kennan and the policy planners on the other. The main difference between these two approaches had been that Clayton had wished for a much more active role by the United States in the whole operation, whereas Kennan was convinced of the necessity that the initiative should be left to Europeans.

The Secretary's political approach was in its essentials not so far removed from the arguments which President Truman had put forward for aid to Greece and Turkey earlier. Although the offer was open to all countries, a government that maneuvered to block the recovery of others could not expect help from the United States, which would also oppose "governments, political parties or groups which seek to per-

[3] See Alexander De Conde, "George Catlett Marshall" in Norman A. Graebner (ed.) , *An Uncertain Tradition* (McGraw, 1961) , p. 254.

petuate human misery in order to profit therefrom politically or otherwise."

But what Marshall appeared to be talking about was a new and enlarged aid program, not a new formula for Europe. The only point in his speech looking toward joint European action came in his repudiation of the Clayton position that the whole onus of leadership should be borne by the United States: "It would," he said, "be neither fitting nor efficacious for this government to undertake to draw up unilaterally a program designed to place Europe on its feet economically . . . The role of this country should consist of friendly aid in the drafting of a European program and of later support of such a program so far as may be practicable for us to do so. The program should be a joint one, agreed to by a number, if not all, of European nations."

As is well known, there was little immediate reaction to this speech in the United States. It was not clear whether it was in fact a gloss on the Truman Doctrine or a welcome return to a joint approach with the Russians. Assuming that it was the latter which was implied, it was not at first opposed by Henry Wallace and other leaders of the American "Left." And because of the fact that no warning had been given, the importance of the speech was not realized by the European embassies in Washington, and it has been said that the British Foreign Minister first had his attention called to the speech and its significance by British journalists.

The Anglo-French consultations entered into on Ernest Bevin's initiative were followed by a preliminary meeting with the Russians, at which it finally became clear that the latter would accept nothing except direct bilateral arrangements for assistance from the United States.[4] In consequence the British and French went ahead with invitations to a general European conference (from which only Spain and the Soviet Union were excluded) which began on July 12. The Russians finally prevented the Poles and Czechs from attending, and the conference and its Committee for European Economic Cooperation (CEEC), set up to prepare a report for the Americans, mark the beginning of a definite approach to recovery on a Western European basis.

[4] It has been pointed out that in its ultimate form the OEEC was not quite so far removed from what Molotov had insisted on as the original split would imply.

It seems that in their work the CEEC used a memorandum by Clayton based on talks which he and Ambassador Lewis Douglas had had with members of the British Cabinet in the last week in June. This document is unavailable, but some American reactions to the course that had been taken can be seen from the next available paper of the Policy Planning Staff, which is dated July 23, 1947.

This document insisted on the importance both of aiding the establishment of a multilateral clearing system and of reducing tariff and other trade barriers with "the eventual formation of a European Customs Union" as "a long-term objective."

The Policy Planning Staff showed itself alive again to the importance of minimizing the direct intervention of the United States in the economic policies of the different European countries. For this reason it advocated concentrating aid as far as possible in the few key items which would have the maximum immediate effect in promoting European recovery. It thought it possible to choose those branches of economic activity, as for example coal, "the effects of which are apt to relate not just to a single country but to be radiated generally across international borders and to affect the European economy as a whole." Again, it thought it possible to grant assistance not just to individual countries but to groups of European states "acting in concert and taking joint responsibility for the utilization of the commodities received."

The document also shows full awareness of the importance of Germany. Its authors wished to make it plain that the primary objective of American policy was to prevent a recrudescence of German militarism and that the contribution that Germany could make to Europe's recovery must be thought of in the light of this fact. Since the question of the possibility of treating Germany as a whole would be determined by the Council of Foreign Ministers, there was no point in the interim in considering anything but the Western Zones.

Finally, the planners were still much influenced by the importance attached in the United States to the United Nations Organization, and therefore emphasized the point that the Marshall Plan was in full conformity with the spirit of the Charter. While in view of the urgency of the situation it was understandable that the European countries concerned should have found it advisable to inaugurate their discussions through a temporary organization rather than through United Nations bodies, this should not constitute a reason for doubt or discouragement as to the long-run usefulness of the United Nations in this field. "The International Bank, the I.M.F., F.A.O. and the projected I.T.O. may all have significant roles to play in connection with a program for European recovery. In addition, the ECE, although it is not now in a position to undertake the overall coordinating job, may play an important part in enabling Europe to take full advantage of the aid to be extended by the United States." In fact, Trygve Lie, then Secretary-General of the United Nations, had offered the services of the organization for such an aid program. But neither the United States nor the European countries nor the Soviet Union had urged the use of the ECE during the negotiations in June and July. It looks as though the British government in particular was opposed to an attempt to channel aid through the ECE in view of the possibilities this would give to Soviet obstructionism. That is, the British and possibly the Western European countries were reconciled to the fact that any viable program would have to take place without Soviet participation.[5] From the point of view of the United States administration, an important consideration must have been the need to secure congressional assent to any plan for aid. Possibly the unwillingness to use the ECE may have been due to considerations of this kind, and after the passage of the Foreign Assistance Act of 1948 it was generally observed that congressional reaction might have been quite different if the Russians had accepted the invitation to participate, or if the ECE had been the chosen instrument.

It must not be thought that the United States, for its part, had already arrived at any hard and fast conclusions about the details of a recovery plan. But it looks as though there was some American sentiment in favor of it, including either some form of economic federation, or as a minimum definite steps looking in that direction. An outline of American policy sent to Paris for communication to the CEEC mentioned a necessary expansion of intra-European trade, possibly involving American support for some clearing system, and looking to an eventual customs union.

The original CEEC draft, as presented to the principal American representatives at the beginning of September was thought by them to be inadequate both because of the high figure at which the demand for

[5] See David Wightman, *Economic Co-operation in Europe* (London, 1956), pp. 29–32.

aid had been put and because of insufficient attention to its international aspects.

The Americans [we are told] stated that they were not trying to dictate but merely giving their view of what was necessary to win approval by the American people. The probability of acceptance would be greatly enhanced if Europe would plan for a continuous progress toward a workable economy at the end of four years. To achieve this purpose a partial delegation of sovereignty to a central organization might be necessary.

The Americans eventually suggested a list of minimum changes, of which some were accepted. But on their side they agreed that the proposed central organization need be only a consultative one, and instead of a commitment to eliminate trade barriers, they agreed that the thirteen countries involved should set up a study group to consider a customs union.[6]

The CEEC report, as amended, was agreed to by a new session of the original conference on September 22.

This plan did not look to economic union but rather to mutual help both in the direction of trade liberalization and in the coordination of certain resources, for instance in transport, and in the production of energy. The participating countries agreed to set up a continuing organization which would "ensure to the full extent possible by joint action, the realization of the economic conditions necessary to enable the general objectives to which each country has pledged itself to be effectively achieved."

After studies by various committees of the possibilities of United States assistance on a massive scale, definite proposals were made by the administration for financial appropriations to this end. Meanwhile, however, the United States in December had had to vote further emergency aid after the British suspension of convertibility on August 20, 1947.[7]

The Americans made a useful contribution to the negotiations between the European powers during the winter of 1947–48. Clayton in particular helped to persuade some recalcitrant countries that the con-

---

[6] W. C. Mallalieu, "The Origin of the Marshall Plan," *Political Science Quarterly* (December 1958), pp. 492–99.

[7] For the British aspect of U.S. aid policies see William C. Mallalieu, *British Reconstruction and American Policy, 1945–1955* (Scarecrow, 1956).

tinuing organization recommended would indeed be required. The United States would in fact have preferred a stronger organization with a greater degree of initiative in the hands of the Secretary-General. It was largely on British objections that this approach foundered, and these objections tended to make American enthusiasts for European unity particularly suspicious of the British, an attitude which was to have serious repercussions throughout the remainder of the period being discussed. It must be remembered that the Labour Government in Britain was concerned to preserve the fiscal autonomy it thought necessary for its own measures of economic planning and to leave the Sterling Area unimpaired; though at the same time the Sterling Area was sometimes talked of as placing an additional burden on Britain. The Sterling Area's operations were in fact helped by the provision of Marshall aid to Great Britain, which went on in its case until December 1950. But this was something which the administration kept quiet about.

On the political side it was Britain's main objective to see that the United States maintained its footing in Europe. Here, the good relations that developed between Ernest Bevin and Dean Acheson were helpful. On the other hand, there was no meeting of minds between the Secretary of the Treasury, John Snyder, and the British Chancellor of the Exchequer, Stafford Cripps.

Nevertheless, agreement was reached in time for President Truman to sign the Foreign Assistance Act on April 2, and for the European countries to agree to the OEEC convention signed on April 16.

Although Congress took some time to deal with the bill, little of the debate directly concerned its possibilities as an instrument for integrating Europe. The supporters of the measure tended to emphasize the general need to fortify the political stability of the Western European countries. But an amendment that the recipient countries should agree as a condition of aid to form a defensive alliance among themselves was defeated. Indeed, at this time the most vocal opposition came from those who were suspicious of the whole program as being an attempt to undermine the authority of the United Nations.

There was also some discussion about the appropriateness of giving aid to the neutrals in the war whose economies had not been directly damaged; but the administration secured assent to the principle that it should be the contribution of countries to the joint effort that should be the criterion.

It is worth noting that Senator Fulbright, consistently with his previous attitude, did attempt to add to the act a phrase to the effect that "the policy of the people of the United States" was "to encourage the political unification of Europe." He was assured by Senator Lodge that the Foreign Relations Committee had been favorable to this point of view, but had not thought it expedient to put it into the bill. In both Houses there were statements that indicated the attitude of Congress toward this issue. In the Senate, Senator H. Alexander Smith said on March 4: "We all know that the small compartments of Europe for hundreds of years have made difficulties that prevented humane understanding between people by which they could move forward. We have solved this particular problem in America by our economic unity and our political safeguards. Our experience may exert an ultimate influence on Europe or at least a federation of European states which will be responsible." In supporting the Fulbright amendment, Congressman Kersten said on March 31: "It may be too optimistic to hope for a United States of Europe immediately. But this amendment will help to pave the way in the not too distant future."

While the act itself referred to the reduction of trade barriers as one of the objectives of the program, the aid to be given was to be the subject of bilateral agreements, on which Congress indeed insisted. But it was hoped that this requirement of a bilateral agreement between each participating country and the United States could be used as a lever for seeing that it cooperated in the full scope of the program. A more important limitation on the freedom of the participating countries lay in the restoration of a system of licensing for exports in order to ensure that commodities which the United States would not export to Eastern Europe on security grounds would not be supplied from Western Europe. This was in spite of the importance attached by administration witnesses to the need for East-West trade in Europe to be increased if Western European recovery were to get going.

As was made clear in an unpublished history of the Marshall Plan compiled by the State Department in the summer of 1948, the expectation there was that the program would in some respects go beyond the mere letter of the assistance act. In other words, the desire for a considerable measure of European integration was not abandoned despite the ready recognition of the delicacy of the issue about national sover-eignty which meant that the United States had to wait on European initiative: "A divided Europe or lack of cohesion among the countries of Western Europe leaves only two major powers vitally concerned with the area. The political integration of Europe, the rebuilding of European political strength, the assertion by Europe of a major voice in world affairs would go far, in the view of this country, to stabilize international relations throughout the world."

On the other hand, such sentiments by no means implied an aban-donment in other quarters of the full internationalist program. As Mr. Clayton had put it in a broadcast on November 22, 1947: "The Mar-shall Plan, or the European Recovery Program, has to do with the short-term emergency needs of one part of the world. The Inter-national Trade Organization has to do with long-range trade policies and trade of all the world. They are highly complementary and inter-related." And even though the hopes of creating such an organization were destined to be frustrated, there is no doubt that there were pres-sures on the administration to make sure in its handling of the aid pro-gram that the emergency measures taken in Europe were not such as to inhibit this long-term objective.

CHAPTER III

The European Recovery Program, 1947–48

IN A MEMORANDUM ON SEPTEMBER 19, 1947, Mr. Clayton had said that it would be necessary to be reconciled to the setting up of an independent agency for the administration of Marshall aid. Given the relations then existing between Congress and the State Department, this was a recognition of the obvious. Congress established, on April 3, 1948, an agency to be known as the Economic Co-operation Administration (ECA) headed by an administrator of Cabinet rank.[1] He was to keep the Secretary of State informed, and matters arising between him and the Secretary were to be settled where necessary by the President himself. In addition to the staff in Washington, the post of United States Special Representative in Europe was created, and he was to be the principal channel of communication between the American aid administration and the new European organization, the Organization for European Economic Cooperation (OEEC). In addition, there were to be separate ECA missions to the various participating countries.

Paul Hoffman was unanimously confirmed as the administrator of the ECA on April 7. He recruited a staff partly from outside the government but also including some of the principal enthusiasts for a European program from the State Department itself. Averell Harriman resigned as Secretary of Commerce to become the special representative in Paris. The principal organizational difficulty arose in connection with Germany, where the High Commissioner, General Lucius Clay,

[1] The text of the Foreign Assistance Act, of which Title I is referred to as the "Economic Co-operation Act of 1948," is given in *Documents on European Recovery and Defence, March 1947–April 1949* (Royal Institute of International Affairs, 1949), pp. 31–68. Subsequent legislation took the form of amendments to this basic text.

wished to deal directly with the United States government and not through OEEC. In the end, Harriman himself became head of the mission to Germany, with a deputy to act for him at Frankfurt. He had to allay the fears in Europe that the United States authorities in Germany would concentrate too exclusively on their own task there and that too high a proportion of American assistance would be channeled through them.[2]

The OEEC itself came into being on June 5, 1948, and was told by Harriman that it was to produce a coherent program by dove-tailing the various national requirements. It was this request that led to the annual review and the other procedures that came to be associated with the OEEC method of operation.[3]

It was, of course, not sufficient to have secured the authorization of the program from Congress. Appropriations were also required, and in this respect the Report of the Select Committee under Congressman Herter was important.[4]

Two points in this document are worth stressing. In the first place, it illustrates again the prominent position of Germany in American thinking of the time: "It is the belief of the Select Committee that the solution to the problem of preventing the resurgence of aggressive German nationalism is to be found within the pattern of European federation, of which a democratic Germany will be an integral but not a dominating part." It was this which provides the background to the committee's view that steps toward European union had so far been inadequate, and that "every effort should be made now to lay the sound foundation for a more far-reaching economic federation directed toward the necessary objectives." It is obvious, too, that the committee was already seized with the notion that was afterward to be so prominently associated with the name of Jean Monnet, namely that economic integration could be used as a method of imposing some form of political union: "It would appear that any substantial economic union will in fact produce a considerable degree of political federation. It would therefore be desirable to recognize this at the out-

[2] A compromise was reached dividing aid for Germany into two parts; that required to maintain a subsistence level went directly to the military government authorities, the remainder came via the Marshall Plan machinery. For Clay's own account, see Lucius D. Clay, *Decision in Germany* (Doubleday, 1950), pp. 215–26.

[3] See Max Beloff, *New Dimensions in Foreign Policy* (London, 1961), pp. 43–46.

[4] U.S. Select Committee on Foreign Aid, *Final Report on Foreign Aid*, H. Rept. 1845, 80 Cong. 2 sess. (1948).

set and to establish limited political federation capable of administering effectively an economic union." But the committee went beyond this view in its assertion that the absence of a common defense system would tend to make for economic nationalism and therefore act as a brake on political union: "These considerations would argue the prime necessity of a common defensive pact underwritten by the United States as a basic condition for a realistic approach to Western European union." This, of course, had already partially been achieved by the Brussels Treaty of March 17, 1948.

The second point was the lack of clarity about whether Britain should participate integrally in such arrangements: "There is no real inconsistency between close economic cooperation with other European countries and the continuation of Britain's intimate economic ties with the Dominions. . . . The success of the European effort for recovery depends in part upon the United Kingdom actively assuming the responsibilities of her position." On the other hand, the committee recognized that there were limitations on what the United States could do other than to encourage the countries concerned to proceed along the lines it thought most suitable.

Some private observers thought, however, that more could have been done directly. In a widely circulated paper entitled "Union of Western Europe: A Third Centre of Power," Professor Klaus Knorr, of the Yale Institute of International Studies, argued in May 1948 that it was unfortunate that the projected pattern of American aid would tend "to reinforce the artificial independence of the several economies in the region rather than their interdependence. The latter would better have been achieved by assistance in reconstructing particular Western European industries rather than particular countries." But the difficulties were admitted in that the OEEC countries wanted help as independent nations and not as members of a region which at this stage was little more than a geographical entity. Moreover, he went on, "financial aid for projects rather than countries would have been viewed by many Congressmen, though unjustifiably, as planning of the pernicious type. Nevertheless it remains important that the American government endeavor—as the aid program progresses—to make a marginal portion of its aid available for investment projects devised from a regional point of view." With Paul Hoffman and his staff, there entered on the scene the first group of persons in America holding key positions and committed to the view that Europe's course should be in the direction of economic integration. Hoffman himself was predisposed to this view by his own experience in the mass production of the automotive industry, but he seems to have discussed its application to Europe with Jean Monnet as early as 1946.

A view of this kind, as far as the administration was concerned, was largely held by those who looked at the scene in the light of their interpretation of economic history. It was not a popular view with the Treasury, which was still dominated by persons of a universalist bent, such as Frank A. Southard, then the Director of the Office of International Finance. The orthodox State Department view, as represented by people like George Kennan, Paul Nitze, and Livingston Merchant, was also rather a skeptical one. The State Department was after all organized to deal with states separately, and perhaps attached more importance to their enduring national characteristics. At the head of the State Department at the beginning there was still General Marshall, assisted by Robert Lovett, Under Secretary since July 1947, who were both prepared to go along with Hoffman. But a more determined voice made itself heard when Dean Acheson returned to the department as Secretary of State on January 20, 1949. In his first year as Secretary of State, Acheson was regarded as somewhat lukewarm on the integrationist aspect of American policy. He tended, it was thought, to look at things rather in the way the British did, and to stress an Atlantic rather than a European approach. It seems that only in 1950, when the Schuman Plan came forward, did he shift into a more pro-integrationist position.

In these circumstances, the good relations that Hoffman maintained with Marshall and Lovett, and afterwards with Acheson, as well as with John Snyder, the Secretary of the Treasury, were of particular importance. His immediate deputy, Richard Bissell, another enthusiast for integration, was also very important in handling people lower down in the administration.

Hoffman was also perhaps fortunate in the fact that circumstances contrived to give his new department an extraordinarily free hand during the first eighteen months of its existence. The Treasury had been demoted somewhat from the important position it had held in the time of Secretary Morgenthau, and the State Department was mistrusted by Congress, where the pro-integrationist sentiments of the Foreign Relations Committee of the Senate were probably strengthened by the interest in the subject of William Y. Elliott, their chief of staff.

The difficulty was to make this general feeling that this was the right line into an instrument of action. The proposal that grants to European countries should be made conditional on their accepting measures of integration was not accepted. It was rather a question of using the influence that aid gave to those administering it to push in the directions they thought important. At the beginning the group was not very politically minded; it thought in economic terms and vaguely of Europe as a whole. The issues with Britain which were to become so important were not fully perceived, perhaps, until after October 1949.

The weight of the ECA itself depended to a very great extent on the personal competence of its staff and the basic slant in policy was that which resulted from the accumulation of day-to-day decisions rather than from far-reaching policy directives. At that time, as Harlan Cleveland was to put it later: "It seemed possible by a kind of institutional magic suddenly to create a political superstructure in Europe which, once it was established, would then attract to itself sufficient loyalty and authority so that in time it would become something like a federal union." [5]

Among Americans who played an important part in securing support for the integrationist approach to Europe were William Tomlinson,[6] the Paris representative of the United States Treasury from 1948 until his death in April 1955, and his principal assistant Stanley Cleveland. Although Tomlinson's full influence only made itself felt after the launching of the Schuman Plan in 1950, it may be illuminating to say something of his role here.

It is not clear when Tomlinson himself became convinced of the truth of the integrationist doctrine, but it was certainly during the negotiations over the French loans and interim aid in 1946 and 1947

---

[5] H. Field Haviland, Jr. (ed.), *The United States and the Western Community* (Haverford College Press, 1957), p. 112.

[6] On Tomlinson, see the letter in *The Times* (London), April 28, 1955 (the anonymous author was one of Tomlinson's British collaborators); see also the note in *Le Monde* by Raymond Aron on May 6, 1955. Further information has been made available to me by Theodore Geiger and others.

that he first established a close working relationship with Jean Monnet which was to be a principal factor in his subsequent activities. During the first two years of the Marshall Plan, Tomlinson was not particularly to the fore, since he was mainly preoccupied with the problems of France's own recovery. But once the Schuman Plan had been launched, he used his influence with the French to make certain that the proposal would not contain restrictionist and other provisions which would prevent the United States supporting it. He was also important in overcoming the objections of people in his own department in Washington who looked askance at any economic arrangements short of complete multilateralism.

After the outbreak of the Korean War, Tomlinson was deeply involved in the problems of NATO and European rearmament, and especially in helping to convince Washington that the proposed European Defense Community (EDC) would provide the only safe framework for the rearmament of Germany. He was associated with Robert Bowie in backing Ambassador David Bruce when he helped persuade the French to revise their original proposals to ones embodying a restoration of German sovereignty. Tomlinson was also present at the final meeting in August 1954 when the ministerial negotiators of the EDC tried in vain to persuade the French Premier, Mendes-France, to support it. The failure of the French Parliament to ratify the EDC treaty was a great blow to Tomlinson, and the frustration of the intensive work that he had put into the negotiations may have been partially responsible for his early death.

More rewarding was Tomlinson's work in relation to the Coal and Steel Community. Monnet apparently suggested him for the post of the first United States representative to that body,[7] and he was in fact made deputy representative, helping in this capacity to negotiate its first loan from the United States. While other American officials, then as later, were undoubtedly very important, one of them has since written as follows: "I am convinced that they would not have been nearly as influential as they were without the spur and support of Tomlinson's driving energy, ingenuity, and capacity to relate effectively in a personal context to virtually all of the continental leaders—both politicians and public servants—of the European unification movement."[8]

[7] *Washington Post,* April 29, 1955.
[8] In a personal letter to the author.

In addition to encouraging those elements in Europe which thought along the same lines, the ECA enthusiasts had, as we have seen in the case of Tomlinson, to argue with opposition in Washington itself. The principal opposition still came from those favoring a more general approach, that of the world-wide trading and financial agreements and institutions. Two minor lines of opposition argument were also sometimes voiced in this period. The integrationist approach was regarded by some as a product of French escapism, a method by which the French could avoid solving their own pressing economic problems. Secondly, it was argued that the European emphasis was likely to handicap developments within an Atlantic framework. This latter argument was denied then and later by most of those concerned, who argued on the contrary that this was the only way in which to approach the wider question of Atlantic cooperation.

In his speech to the OEEC on July 25, 1948, in which Hoffman called on the member countries to devise a "master-plan of action based upon the full recovery of the European economy by June 30, 1952," when American aid would terminate, he asserted that it was not only a growing conviction that the interests of the United States demanded that "Europe should again become a living workable and independent economic and political organization," but that there had at the same time been a "growing conviction that this goal" could not be "set in the frame of an old picture or traced on an old design."

"Each participating nation," he said, "looking at the operations of its own national life, must face up to readjustments to satisfy the requirements of a new world. These readjustments cannot be made in course of national action along the old separatist lines. They can only be accomplished if each nation seeks its new goal in terms of the economic capacity and the economic strength of Europe as a whole."

It has been suggested that the ECA could have done still more to make this policy effective. Senator Fulbright has written "the United States might well have exploited the opportunity provided by the European Recovery Program to push the hesitant nations towards political federation as well as economic cooperation, but all proposals to this effect were rejected by the United States government at the time." [9]

Two points may perhaps be made at this stage. In the first place,

[9] J. W. Fulbright, "For a Concert of Free Nations," *Foreign Affairs* (October 1961).

there was a general sense in the administration that movements toward the reshaping of Europe must come from Europeans, as indeed they eventually did, and that American pressure should be limited to supporting such initiatives. The administration was reluctant to appear to be dictating to sovereign European governments, and was at most willing to use its influence to try and bring recalcitrant countries into line with the majority of OEEC members. Although this general attitude was occasionally abandoned, most notably, as we shall see, in the case of the European Defense Community, it was, taking the period as a whole, substantially adhered to.

In the second place, very few of the national economic recovery programs to which such stimulus was given by Marshall aid were seriously altered in the interests of knitting the European economy together more tightly. Changes were, of course, made to permit agreement on the division of aid and in the field of removing trade barriers, but few decisions on investments or on the general patterns of the rebuilt economies were based on the assumptions of close integration. It has been suggested that this itself suggests a limitation on the commitment of the United States to an integrationist program for Europe at this time. But one must also take into account the fact that the programs were largely the affair of the aid missions to the different countries, and that these naturally tended to identify themselves with the country for which they were responsible rather than with the more remote objective of the program as a whole. In this sense the American authorities in Germany only exemplify an extreme case of the common attitude.

It must also be remembered that in dealing with the recovery program the American administration had to fit it into its general policy in foreign affairs, of which the most obvious feature was the growing need to resist Soviet pressure. The first year of activity of the ECA coincided with the struggle symbolized by the Berlin airlift and with the negotiations that led from the Brussels Treaty of March 17, 1948, to the North Atlantic Treaty of April 4, 1949.

A close observer, writing shortly afterwards, wrote that "very early in 1949 the ECA ceased pressing the member countries to prepare an overall four-year 'master-plan' for Europe which had seemed so important and promising in 1948 and had served the purpose of focusing attention on many of the area's problems, because the plans for the individual nations appeared to be developing along lines of national autarky and promised to result in a Europe less, rather than more, economically unified." [10]

On the other hand, the ECA did exert its influence in two directions that appeared hopeful—greater freedom of payments and limited customs unions. In regard to the first of these, the achievement of a multilateral system of payments within Europe was to some extent impeded in the American view by the excessive caution of the United Kingdom, arising out of its concern for the impact of such a development on the position of sterling. Some pressure on the United Kingdom was sought in the form of a deliberate leak of the American plan that had been worked out during the summer, and some progress was made.

Meanwhile, earlier in the year, Congress had debated the extension of the European Recovery Program for a further year, and various congressmen had again expressed their view that economic unity was insufficient of itself.

"If," said Senator Thomas, "we cannot bring about new ideals and decent notions in regard to trade, if we leave the notion in Europe that every nation is to be antagonistic to other nations, that it is only in economic unity and not in political unity that they can go forward, there will be the same rivalry which has always resulted in war."

Senator Fulbright doubted the reassuring statement made by Senator Vandenberg that Europe had made great progress toward integration.

Last year [he said] I sought to have the objective of a European federation incorporated into the authorization of the European Recovery Program. I was unsuccessful. This year in committee I offered an amendment seeking the same objective. The committee accepted the word "unification" but would not accept the word "political." They rejected the cement. For more than two years I have been urging our government to encourage, frankly and positively, the political unification of Europe. Our government has not seen fit to do so. It has been said by those who resist this policy that it would give substance to the Communist charge of American imperialism.

[10] Gardner Patterson, *Survey of United States International Finance* (Princeton University Press, 1950), p. 135. For a critical account of ECA policies from a mutilateralist standpoint, see William Adams Brown, Jr. and Redvers Opie, *American Foreign Assistance* (Brookings Institution, 1953), Chap. 7. On p. 273 of this work they remark: "During the period of the recovery program the problems raised by the integration or unification of Western Europe were not thought through by its American advocates and . . . the objective sought was never clearly defined."

But, he argued, imperialism would mean dividing Europe whereas what we are asking for is to encourage its unification. "A basic fallacy," he continued, "in the philosophy of the ECA and our foreign policy makers in the State Department is the sharp distinction they make between economic and political affairs, and the undue significance they attach to what they call economic cooperation and recovery." He attacked the theory that recovery itself would aid the process of integration.[11]

It is probably true that there was a distinction here between the line of thought followed by Senator Fulbright and the less political inspiration of the ECA at that time. By the summer of 1949 the ECA believed that it had achieved the first objective of American policy, namely preventing a European collapse. It now switched to a drive to increase Europe's economic efficiency by promoting increasing trade and competition, and in speeches and press conferences in the late summer Hoffman used the words "economic unification." He informed the OEEC on September 3 that from next year "aid would be distributed not according to need as in the past, but according to the performance of the participating countries in effectively utilizing the aid and realizing the objectives of . . . the Economic Cooperation Act." And in fact the ECA earmarked $150 million out of the 1949–50 appropriations as a special fund for use primarily in order to underwrite genuine efforts at liberalizing European trade and payments.

The underlying philosophy of the ECA operation was seemingly worked out by staff members between the summer of 1949 and the following spring. The first of these documents was entitled "The Problem of Western Europe's Competitive Position in the World Economy and Its Remedy" and was dated July 19, 1949. This ambitious paper begins with an examination of the economic history of Europe with a view to discovering why the industrial revolution had failed to have the same far-reaching effects in Europe as in the United States. It finds a decline in the European growth by the end of the nineteenth century and that this has been met by resort to monopoly and restrictionism, with the result that in the interwar period "the intensification of eco-

---

[11] The amending act, approved on April 19, 1949, included in the preamble the declaration that it was "the policy of the people of the United States to encourage the unification of Europe."

nomic nationalism in Western Europe itself became a contributing factor to the widening disparities from which it arose."

All the measures to which the European countries resorted, particularly after the great depresssion, "tended to entrench the very maladjustments whose effects they were designed to mitigate," and the decline of both internal and external competition removed the incentives to increasing efficiency and productivity—a process partially masked in the interwar period by the improvement in the terms of trade, but now fully revealed. Europe requires important exports to pay for what it needs, particularly with the disappearance of much of its revenue on invisible account. But it can only export to protected areas because of its lack of competitiveness with the United States economy.

It now seemed to the authors that a new opportunity existed, partially because some of the social stratification and traditional patterns of consumption which had hampered economic growth in Europe had been swept away as a result of the war and occupation. And the desire for higher standards was being accelerated by the increasing knowledge of the American standard of living. But the new goals could only be attained by fundamental alterations in the economic structure as a whole.

In a second section the authors went into Europe's problems in terms of economic theory, explaining economic growth primarily in terms of a deepening and widening market which permits the maximum advantages to be obtained from a division of labor. In Europe itself this extension of the market was inhibited by national boundaries, not only because of the protectionist devices used but because they produced an inhibitory effect on entrepreneurs, who were unwilling to undertake the risks of doing business across national borders. Because the markets were so small, intensity of competition and the spirit of competition were limited: "This is surely a major part of the explanation of the lifeless moribund character of contemporary Western European capitalism."

What was required was something basically different:

. . . the formation of a single pervasive and highly competitive domestic market in Western Europe of sufficient size and scope to support mass production for mass consumption. This requires the elimination of barriers to the free movement of goods, persons and ultimately capital. It requires the final conquest of noncommercial production and consumption by the market. It entails the abandonment of governmental and private restrictionist and protectionist practices and the end of open or covert autarkies of a local or national character.

Western Europe presented certain advantages for the creation of a new market of this kind because of the density of its population and the fact that transfer costs were consequently low. While to produce an actual rate of growth comparable to that of the United States might seem a remote objective, what could be achieved was an improvement in the rate of growth comparable to the American improvement. It was therefore essential, if the benefits of American aid were not to be short-lived, that the European Recovery Program help provide the necessary structural changes: "The basic disparity in Western Europe today is the fact that the particular size of the unit necessary for its continued, successful existence in the medium of the world economy is larger than the actual size of the existing political units."

It was no use expecting automatic remedies. If people merely waited for what time would bring, the result would be the sterile unification of a Communist solution. Instead, a major conscious effort was needed to "induce precisely those structural changes and that type of liberal solution which would be acceptable to the United States and would perpetuate free, though perhaps novel, economic and political institutions."

A third section discussed the obstacles to action and the first steps that needed to be taken, going into some detail on the methods under discussion for completing trade liberalization and for new multilateral payments arrangements, with reference to what American aid could do to cushion the transitional period. More significant for the line of thinking that was being followed was the assertion that some institutional development was required so as to prevent governments maintaining or re-imposing trade barriers in order to offset the internal effects on their economies of the measures of liberalization now suggested.

What the authors suggested was the establishment of an Intra-European Commerce Commission modeled on the United States Interstate Commerce and Federal Trade Commissions, and having, like its American counterpart, quasi-executive and judicial powers.

This commission should be a truly impartial international body composed not of national representatives, but of outstanding individuals chosen by lot from a panel nominated by the governments, and serving for a fixed term of years. The agreed principles in commercial policy that the commission should enforce would be embodied in the convention creating it. The right of a judicial appeal from its decisions and actions to the International Tribunal at The Hague should be provided.

In relation to this new commission, which would be a sort of executive, the OEEC would act in the capacity of a legislature, drawing up a set of basic commercial principles and practice. In this way, it was argued, a body of international law and precedent could gradually be established in the field of European commercial policy which it would become increasingly difficult for the participating countries to ignore or circumvent. Since the commission would not operate on a world-wide most-favored-nation basis, it should not be doomed to ineffectiveness, pending the solution of the world dollar problem. Furthermore, the initial surrender of national sovereignty entailed by its creation would not be so great as to be unacceptable.

It was also the case that quite apart from what might be done by such a commission, a high degree of coordination of national economic policies in Western Europe would have to be undertaken. While the first steps might be taken later on, insuperable obstacles might arise because of the unwillingness of participating countries to open up their economies to unpredictable impacts generated by their neighbors' actions, particularly in the field of money and prices. Or to put it more positively, the proposed removal of economic barriers between the countries of Western Europe might create a need for the coordination of their policies so extensive as to be beyond the capacities of normal diplomacy or of intergovernmental committee procedures such as those of the OEEC. And if this were to prove the case, the OEEC and the proposed commission might well be the nucleus around which other supranational functional agencies could be built. This, in effect, it was argued, was the only possible road to economic union. It was no good expecting the nations of Western Europe completely to surrender their economic sovereignties in a single dramatic action like the renunciation of feudal privileges by the French noblesse in 1789. The strength and durability of the modern national state would prevent it. The economic union of Europe, if it were to come about at all, would have to be built up gradually in the interstices of the national states through the creation of functional institutions able successfully to grapple with specific problems, outside the jurisdiction of, or beyond the capacity of, the national states. Only when these new organs had gained strength, experience, and stability could a frontal attack be made on the sovereignty of the national state. For at that point the problem would be one only of political union.

This document, which was signed by Theodore Geiger, H. van Buren Cleveland, and John Hulley, was followed on October 15 by another paper from the first two authors entitled "The Economic Integration of Western Europe." Since this document is still classified, the extent to which it added to the argument can only be gathered from quotations from it in the book by Harry B. Price, *The Marshall Plan and Its Meaning*.[12] It seems to have gone into more detail on the relationship between such economic thinking and the problem of Germany. "What solution is there" asked the authors, "to the German problem outside of membership in a Western European union?" And again, "membership in a union might well [they say] be the one method for making Europeans out of Germans and for harnessing their talents for management and production in a better cause than German nationalism." The authors saw as the "crucial and compelling reason for Western European Union" the fact that it provided "the main hope for a regeneration of Western European civilization and for a new period of stability and growth."

A third document, entitled "How Far Can the ERP Achieve the Objectives of United States Policy in Western Europe?" was submitted on April 26, 1950, by the same two authors, but this is also not available.[13]

In the second of the documents, the authors had pointed out that persons most familiar with attitudes in Congress were afraid that the continuation of aid at the minimum necessary level could not be expected unless Western European countries had clearly started on the road to economic unity. A message to this effect was sent by the ECA

12 Cornell University Press, 1955. The document in question is quoted on p. 121.
13 For a public summary of the views of this school of thought, see Theodore Geiger and H. van Buren Cleveland, *Making Western Europe Defensible*, National Planning Association, Planning Pamphlet 74 (August 1951).

to its European regional office in October 1949. The same message emphasized the urgency of getting something done soon, since as aid tapered off, the shocks inseparable from measures of economic integration would be more difficult to cushion. It was decided that Hoffman himself should make an important speech to the OEEC, emphasizing these points. The first draft of this seems to have gone beyond what the State Department was prepared to accept as a statement of American policy, and references to the "unification" of Europe were removed, the word "integration" being substituted.

These verbal changes implied to some extent a repudiation of the rather far-reaching line of thought in the documents that had just been analyzed. The State Department at this time was still by no means committed to integrationist ideas, and Hoffman's speech, while radical enough about the desirability of freeing the movement of goods, was not concerned with anything not related directly to the economic problem that Europe faced.

Hoffman began his speech by noting the presence for the first time of representatives of the German Republic as full partners in the OEEC. Since 1947 he pointed out, both Communists and cynics had been confounded by the proof given that it was possible both to start economic recovery in Western Europe and to lay foundations for security against attack on the Atlantic community.

Two major tasks now lay ahead; the first was to balance Europe's dollar accounts. The second, he went on, "and to say this is why I am here—is to move ahead on a far-reaching program, to build in Western Europe a more dynamic expanding economy which will promise steady improvement in the conditions of life for all its people. This I believe means nothing less than integration of the Western European economy."

After discussing the financial problem, he moved on to explain in familiar terms the advantages of the creation of a single permanent freely trading area. This "massive change in the economic environment," was, he went on, a "vital objective." "It was to this," he said, "that Secretary Marshall pointed in the speech which sparked Europe to new hope and new endeavor. It was on this promise that the Congress of the United States enacted the ECA Act."

While not dismissing the difficulties in the way of such a policy,

Hoffman argued that the alternative would be the setting into motion again of "the vicious cycle of economic nationalism." Its consequences would be "the cumulative narrowing of markets, the further growth of high-cost protected industries, the mushrooming of restrictive controls, and the shrinkage of trade into the primitive pattern of bilateral barter."

Hoffman showed that he was prepared to consider both such steps toward the common goal as the OEEC countries might take together, and special arrangements between particular groups of countries. But these should be in harmony with the wider objectives of European integration. He emphasized once more the urgency of beginning a program of integration at once. There was only a very short time still remaining during which American aid would be available; "the people and the Congress of the United States, and, I am sure a great majority of the people of Europe, have instinctively felt that economic integration is essential if there is to be an end to Europe's recurring economic crises. A European program to this end—one which should show real promise of taking this great forward step successfully— would, I strongly believe, give new impetus to American support for carrying through into 1952 a joint effort toward lasting European recovery."

While Mr. Hoffman did not stray outside his economic brief, he allowed his audience to catch a glimpse of a higher political purpose:

> We are together playing for high stakes in this program. The immediate goal is a solidly based prosperity for an economically unified Western Europe—a goal which President Truman reaffirmed to me just before I left Washington. Beyond that lies what has been the hope of all men of good will during your lifetime and mine, an enduring peace founded on justice and freedom. That high hope can be realized if we, the people of the free world, continue to work together and stick together.

It will be seen that whereas Hoffman accepted the economic philosophy of the ECA staff papers, neither he nor the State Department accepted their suggestion for new institutional devices. He seemed to be thinking in terms of what the existing governments could do, and it was on these governments in the next few months that he exercised decisive pressure in favor of trade liberalization and the freeing of the exchanges. An all night session with Sir Stafford Cripps in December 1949 proved necessary in order to persuade him that Hoffman could not ask Congress for more money unless Britain were willing to dismantle still further the controls on its external economic relations.

Just before the end of the year an attempt was made, supported by ECA, to strengthen the authority of OEEC by having more frequent and perhaps even continuous participation of representatives of Cabinet rank, and by acquiring as its permanent head an outstanding political figure. The British were prepared to accept more frequent ministerial meetings, but disagreed strongly with the United States over the idea of a political Secretary-General.

With regard to economic integration "the British Government quickly made it clear that, while it supported the general ideas of the Americans and would cooperate, it could not fully integrate its economy with that of Europe because of its responsibilities to the sterling area and the Commonwealth." [14]

It was in these months that the Americans began to accept, though with some reluctance at first, the conclusion implicit in Hoffman's speech that it might be necessary to proceed with something less than the OEEC grouping. There was a plan for a French association with Italy and the Benelux countries, though the differences in tariff policies were an obstacle. But by the end of the year something more critical had come up in that the Americans had made it clear that they "favored the integration of Germany in an economically united Western bloc." [15] A possible bringing together of the resources of the Ruhr and of Lorraine in an industrial pool had been canvassed by some Frenchmen of the Monnet circle in wartime London. But such ideas had dropped out of sight between 1945 and 1949. What now brought them to a head was the American decision that German recovery could not and should not be held down. It was the American view, that "by interlocking the capital structure of French and German industry, French military and political fears could be allayed without blocking Germany's capacity to recover." On the other hand, the French were very doubtful about the ability of their heavy industries to face free competition from Germany. The discussions therefore, as far as the Europeans were concerned, tended to hinge on Britain

---

[14] Patterson, *op. cit.*, p. 144.
[15] *Ibid.*, p. 145.

rather than Germany. Indeed, it appeared that only the participation of Britain could make it certain that Germany would not dominate a bloc of this kind if it were created.

But before steps in this direction were taken, there were achievements in the more general field—a sharp reduction in import quotas and the establishment of the European Payments Union. The second report of the OEEC in February 1950 stressed the importance of establishing such a Payments Union and of the desirability of allocating a part of the available American aid to facilitate this achievement. There was, as a decisive point in the negotiations, a meeting between the ECA representatives and the British and French delegations to the OEEC at which a commitment was given that such aid would be forthcoming. It then remained the task of the ECA to convince the American State and Treasury Departments of the desirability of fulfilling this undertaking. This involved also an important amendment to the aid legislation and Hoffman received authority from Congress to withhold not less than six hundred million dollars of the next year's aid allocation "to encourage the aggressive pursuit of a program of liberalized trade." [16] It was known that the British had put up some resistance to the scheme as originally propounded, and Britain consequently came in for some criticism from Congress. But agreement was reached and the European Payments Union was formally launched on July 7, 1950.

In the course of the hearings on the extension of the European Recovery Program in 1950, both Acheson and Hoffman had to deal with questions from members of Congress who still felt that the United States should bring more pressure on the Europeans to integrate their economies and to unite politically. The view of the administration, as expressed by Acheson, was that the two concepts of economic and political integration, which were often confused with each other, should be separated. His view was that the United States would look with favor on the political unification of Europe, but that such unification was not a prerequisite of progress in the economic field, and that it was not something that the United States could force on the Europeans against their own judgment.

The House of Representatives amended the act so as to include among the objectives of American policy the encouragement of "the

[16] Economic Cooperation Act of 1950, approved June 5, 1950.

economic unification and federation of Europe." But at the conference stage the words "and federation" were deleted, partly in response to the administration's objections and partly because the announcement of the Schuman Plan suggested the possibility of progress along a different line.

Quite apart from these familiar arguments about the essence of this policy, there were two other possible lines of attack. In the first place there were some congressional objections in regard to the compatibility of the program on the economic side with the general aim of securing a world in which there would be no forms of economic discrimination. The administration, however, defended the program in this respect as being a step on the way to full multilateralism.

The other difficulty arose from the renewed discussion about what could be done on an Atlantic footing. Statements by Acheson in the early summer on the possibility of closer association between the United States and Canada on the one hand and the OEEC on the other could be and were frequently interpreted in Europe as being pointers in the direction of Atlantic unity. During the year an attempt was made by a group of Americans favorable to this approach, the "Atlantic Union Committee," to secure congressional approval of a proposal that the President should invite the signatories of the North Atlantic Treaty to a "federal convention" to discuss the possibility of establishing a North Atlantic Federal Union. Brief hearings on this project were held, but it did not reach the floor of the House.

If some people in Britain thought that this Atlantic "solution" might be a way of avoiding the choice of a European orientation, most Americans regarded the two prospects as complementary ones. In the course of the European Recovery Program hearings, Ambassador Harriman said: "I am hopeful that more steps will be taken, not alone in the OEEC organization, but in the Council of Europe and overall. There is the concept of the North Atlantic community, the North Atlantic Pact, which is very much of a welding influence in Europe. In other words, participation of the United States in the North Atlantic Pact, and the concept of the North Atlantic community, is a very important factor in getting these countries together."

In the second half of the year, when the European countries had adopted a new code of liberalization and when Europeans were discussing the various other schemes proposed for breaking down the intra-European barriers to trade, the United States, apart from its close interest in the Schuman Plan, took a more passive attitude in view of its increasing preoccupation with the problems of rearmament, after the outbreak of the Korean War in June.

CHAPTER IV

Prelude to New Policies

TO FOLLOW THE POLITICAL DEVELOPMENTS from 1950 onward, it is necessary to retrace our steps to the end of 1947, at which time the United States was still unwilling to consider an Atlantic alliance. Ernest Bevin went ahead with the idea of a Western European alliance, which as we have seen was eventually embodied in the Brussels Treaty of March 17, 1948 in the professed expectation that the United States would eventually participate. Negotiations for an Atlantic alliance in fact began in July, and, assisted by the evidence of Soviet pressure provided by the Berlin blockade, a treaty was concluded on April 4, 1949. While it is well known that Bevin's thinking on matters of this kind was hostile to any idea of acting within a purely European framework, the American approach was a more complicated one.

Some guidance regarding the state of mind in the United States in the early summer of 1948 may be had from the paper by Professor Klaus Knorr already referred to.[1] In this paper, which is said to have been influential in some official quarters, Knorr called attention to the apparent trend toward consolidation in Western Europe, which might eventually produce a third center of power. American policy toward it should be guided by the views held on how it would affect American interests. But in fact there had been, as he noted, an almost unanimous expression of approval of the Brussels pact. It was not, however, clear as yet whether its conclusion meant the foundation of a Western European union of the kind that much American opinion thought to be desirable.

From the point of view of the United States the first important

[1] "Union of Western Europe: A Third Centre of Power."

49

thing to observe was, in Professor Knorr's view, the fact that Britain had now reversed its attitude toward closer cooperation in Europe. (This, it will be seen, went rather further than a knowledge of Mr. Bevin's mind would have justified.) But his main point was probably sound enough: "Britain and the rest of Western Europe are no longer afraid of each other; both now fear the Soviet colossus."

Professor Knorr then gave reasons for believing that something less than a full federal union might be more feasible. Of such a Western association, Britain, France, and the Low Countries would be the indispensable nucleus. After considering the list of other countries whose relations with this nucleus would have to be worked out, he concludes with a reference which shows the degree of hesitation in American thinking about Germany:

> Only the British, American, and French zones of Germany are in a position to join a Western union if they are invited to do so. The de facto division of Germany into West and East is accepted as a political datum, since the Soviet Union is unlikely to relinquish its control over Eastern Germany unless such a step was a preliminary to gaining control over the entire country, and since neither the Western European countries nor the United States are likely to fight for a re-unified Germany.

Although Germany would be important to such an association, Knorr recognizes the difficulties. First, it would seem to accept the de facto division of Germany—accepting the de jure division would lead to entry into a Western union being strongly opposed by many Germans. On the other hand, to identify such a union with German irredentism would be dangerous. For practical purposes it would be essential to keep open an invitation to the Eastern Germans, and perhaps to the Finns, Poles, Czechs, and Hungarians as well. Clearly the full implications of the division of Europe were not altogether being faced at this time. On the other hand, Knorr showed considerable realism in his acceptance of the fact that the Western Europeans had no wish to become satellites of North America, and in particular that the Western European Left did not wish to be pushed into the position of having to choose between a Soviet dominated and an American dominated bloc.

There were important aspects of policy concerning which these Western European countries should seek to reach agreement; the relation of individual members to their colonial possessions and a decision regarding what to do about the relations between Europe and the British Commonwealth. Here Knorr argued that a compromise solution which allowed Britain "to remain a part of both systems, a Western association and the Commonwealth, should be possible."

He realized that the whole problem was one which would have to be tackled in two phases. The countries of Western Europe could not hope to improve much in mobilized power before the end of the Recovery Program in 1952. To impose defense burdens on these countries before that date would slow down their economic recovery, and by weakening the influence of the center parties make the whole area more vulnerable to Soviet penetration. But after 1952 there should be a basis for greater preparedness on the military side as well.

When Knorr goes into the economic aspects of the matter, he again returns to the question of making a special provision for Commonwealth relationship, saying "while the two systems could be interlocked in principle, by introducing the European union into the Ottawa system, this solution is hardly feasible, if only because the United States would violently oppose it." On the other hand, the United States had accepted at Havana the idea of a Western European low-tariff club.[2] In conclusion, Knorr refers to the long-run desirability for basic strategic reasons of a united Western Europe. The hope would be not that it would become an instrument of American policy but that it would have a balancing effect as between the two world powers, while itself continuing within a broadly democratic tradition. In other words, Knorr was pursuing a line of argument based on hopes of avoiding what came to be called in the 1950's a bipolar world. Furthermore, he saw the advantage of preventing the Americans from being involved in too great detail in the affairs of particular European countries, which could only result in friction.

At this time agreement without Britain seemed impossible: "Britain must be the king-pin of any union that is to mature into impressive strength." On the other hand, about Germany there was, as we have seen, some hesitation: "It is too late now for the United States to

---

[2] The final act of the Havana Conference, signed on March 24, 1948, made exceptions for customs unions to the general rule of nondiscrimination. In August 1948, the General Agreement on Tariffs and Trade of October 30, 1947, was amended to conform more closely with the Havana decisions. The amendment was more widely drawn than the traditional customs union clauses of exception to most-favored-nation treatment and was probably intended to cover not merely Benelux but any wider grouping that might come about in Europe.

further Western unification at the expense of Germans by handing a quasi-colonial Trizonia over to Western Europe as a sort of dowry." But it is now improbable that a unified Germany by agreement between the four occupying powers is possible: "And this realization is clearing the way for reorganizing Western Germany as a going concern and for bringing her into the Western camp. The best way of bringing her in can be evolved only in the course of painstaking negotiations with France and Germany and after a painstaking assessment of political trends in Germany itself." In particular, it had to be borne in mind that the Russians would retain the possibility of offering dazzling prizes to Germany as the price of their abandoning a Western alignment. So that while it was desirable not to press the Western Europeans too hard in the interests of the Germans, so also the Germans themselves must willingly follow the line of development agreed upon.

These doubts, which may be considered fairly representative of the time, were gradually removed in the ensuing twelve months as the division in Europe hardened. And by the time of the Council of Foreign Ministers' meeting in Paris in May–June 1949, the majority view in the United States already looked toward some kind of Western European political union under a general Atlantic guarantee. The main pressure on the political side, as on the economic, was thus in respect of the equivocal position of Britain. A critical discussion of the American viewpoint was, it would seem, set out by George Kennan in a paper of that time. Apparently he suggested a form of organization under which a continental axis based on France and Germany, and more or less identical with what came to be the "Six" of little Europe, should co-exist with a United Kingdom-United States-Canadian axis which might also include countries on the Atlantic periphery of Europe such as Norway, Iceland, and Portugal. The main advantage of this alternative, as Kennan saw it at the time, was that the continental European grouping might still have had an attraction for the countries of central and east-central Europe, while it was out of the question that they would be permitted by the Russians to engage themselves in any organization which included the United States and Britain. In this sense it marked something of a return to the original plans put forward by Rostow in the early part of 1946.

The scheme would have the secondary advantage of making Canada's position easier than if Britain went into a continental grouping, and it would also prevent the United Kingdom from acting as a brake on the closer integration of the continental group, which needed to be as strong as possible if it were to provide the solution of the problem of holding in check the ambitions of a recovering Germany. Kennan's influence had, however, waned sharply with Acheson's assumption of the Secretaryship of State. Acheson was concentrating on the immediate task of building up anti-Communist alliances, but he allowed the department to sound out opinion in Europe on the Kennan scheme. The French were hostile as usual to any arrangements which seemed likely to place Great Britain in closer relations with the United States than themselves. The British too were unwilling to contemplate a tight grouping on the continent from which they would be excluded, while being, of course, unwilling to enter one themselves. Finally, the European Affairs Bureau of the State Department was favorable to the French approach to the situation, and wished to use such influence as was available to bring Britain into a continental European union. The department was less concerned than Kennan with the longer-range prospects with regard to Eastern Europe—an area which for practical purposes it had already written off.

Before the 1949 Foreign Minister's meeting it was possible to argue against bringing Germany into a tight organization of an Atlantic kind from another point of view, for at this time some of the people in the State Department took the view that a substantial withdrawal of Soviet forces from central Europe would be so highly beneficial in its effects that it would be worth withdrawing American forces from Europe if this were the price of bringing it about:

> We did not [writes Paul Nitze] see how the re-unification of Germany in a form acceptable to the Bonn Government could be prevented if Russian military forces were not directly present in support of the Eastern regime. Far from wishing Germany or any other part of central Europe to become part of NATO, it was our thought that the influence of the NATO powers would be directed to keeping central Europe a buffer area, incapable of disturbing the security of the West or of challenging the East.[3]

[3] Paul Nitze, "Alternatives to NATO," in Klaus Knorr (ed.), *Nato and American Security* (Princeton University Press, 1959), pp. 268–69.

From the summer of 1949 such talk of "disengagement," as it came to be called, seemed increasingly unreal in the light of American military thinking. But the final political lines were only gradually drawn from 1950 onward.

It was not at this time possible to say that the Americans had a coherent German policy. Whereas the Russians had seen from the beginning that a conquered country could be rebuilt as part of one's own alliance system, the Americans were slower off the mark. They were torn between *hoping* for an agreement with the Russians which would permit them to let the Germans go into some kind of reunited but disarmed Germany, and *expecting* a long period of conflict when they would wish to have as many Germans as possible on their own side. These two policies did not seem necessarily contradictory if one accepted the fact that they were based on different time scales. It was still felt possible that the power factor in Europe could so alter that the whole of Germany would swing over to the West.

If it were a question of bringing the Germans finally onto one's own side, then of course the military factor was bound to come in; and from the time of the Brussels Treaty at least, thought was being given behind the scenes, both to the possible necessity for West German rearmament and to the desirability of creating integrated European forces for defense. But what was happening in these years was that people in America, as elsewhere, were responding to situations as they arose rather than making up their minds on long-term issues. And where there appeared to be some logical contradiction between policies, this was not stressed because, for practical reasons, one wanted as many people as possible to go along with the policy adopted.

As far as can be seen, there was not at this time any clear conception of Germany as presenting a problem for which alternative solutions were possible. That is to say there was not, as there was to be in 1951–52, talk of a possible bargain with the Russians, offering them a reunited but neutral Germany as an alternative to a Western Germany fully integrated into an Atlantic alliance.

Such a possibility could, indeed, only be considered when more progress had been made with reconstituting a Western German state within the general framework of Western policy. The interesting question here is to account for the speed with which the process commended itself to American minds. For there was certainly a difference between the Americans on the one hand and most Europeans, and more particularly the British, on the other. It must seem in retrospect as though the wartime determination to leave Germany in the condition postulated for it under the Morgenthau Plan should be treated as an aberration from the main line of American thinking. The Americans, having suffered less at German hands, had less reason for allowing revengeful feelings to cloud their view of what was practical in the light of new concerns. A decision that Germany should be made viable was bound to be pressed for by the occupation authorities themselves, and there was an advantage for them in the fact of General Clay's vigor and prestige. Again, this might reasonably seem to Congress the only way in which the major financial burden on the nonmilitary side of America's involvement in Europe could be liquidated within a reasonably short space of time.

Before this policy could be taken further, it was of course necessary that the whole of the American governmental machine should work in reasonable harmony, and it is significant that it was about 1950 that the various difficulties of reorganization of the immediate postwar period were solved. The State Department had reshaped itself to meet the new demands, and the initiative in foreign policy, which had been shared with the White House, the Treasury, the military departments, and the ECA, was recovered. Although important figures like Acheson and Harriman were still fairly cautious in their approach to the problems of European unity, it does seem to be the case that from about 1950 it was the State Department itself that became the principal exponent of supporting the movement as conducive to the objectives of American foreign policy itself.

Because this change in the Washington scene roughly coincided with the initiation of the Schuman Plan, it is not easy in the absence of detailed documentation to work out the exact relationship between the acceleration of events in Europe and American thought and action. Since this study concentrates on the American side of the story, it is perhaps worth re-emphasizing the fact that the initiative itself was a European one and that the creation in the 1950's of the European communities must be regarded as an achievement of the European peoples themselves, just as the philosophy by which it was justified was the product of European thinking.

CHAPTER V

The European Coal and Steel Community

WE HAVE SEEN THAT although leading personages in the ECA talked freely about European integration, what was actually done was more in the direction of trade "liberalization" and had little direct political relevance. Quite different were the French proposals put forward on May 9, 1950, for a joint authority to look after the whole of the French and German coal and steel production also to be open to other European countries. This, the "Schuman Plan," as it came to be called, was the first move toward creating "supranational" authorities in Europe. And with its rejection by Britain it also became the foundation of what was to be the "little Europe" of the "Six" (France, Germany, Italy, Belgium, the Netherlands, and Luxembourg).

It is clear that the origins of the Schuman Plan are to be found in France and that the person principally responsible for the idea was Jean Monnet, at that time the head of the French Planning Organization. The political possibility had been present ever since Schuman had replaced Georges Bidault as French Foreign Minister in July 1948. But the issues that the Plan was meant to tackle had, of course, been present in people's minds ever since the war in the question of the Ruhr. Negotiations about the long-term control of the Ruhr industries began in February–March 1948, and these led to the Ruhr Agreement of April 1949. The French had not been satisfied with the agreement, which they considered gave an inadequate control over German production; and the international authority for the Ruhr never became an institution of any real importance. It was subordinate to the occupying powers, and as we have seen, from their point of view, particularly from the American point of view, the economic recovery and political rehabilitation of Germany became an in-

creasingly important objective. Indeed, there had been some suggestions from the American side, from the autumn of 1949, that the two
policies might be reconciled by extending the idea of the Ruhr authority to the coal and steel production of Western Europe as a whole,
though at this time the British were unwilling to have the current negotiations with the Germans for the restitution to them of a measure
of political self-determination complicated by the inclusion of the further long-term considerations.[1]

But ideas of this kind were obviously in circulation, and Monnet
himself has given some of the credit to William Clayton. It was in talks
with Clayton, he said, "that the germ of the idea developed that Ruhr
production should be utilized not only for Germany or as the result of
bilateral arrangements, but that it should contribute to the production of the whole of Europe." [2]

But the French acted quite independently when it came to the point,
and Ambassador Bruce himself was only informed after the Cabinet
had made the basic decision. At this time, Secretary Acheson was also
in Paris on the way to London to discuss the question of the control of
German industry, and he was at first hesitant about the plan in view
of the lack of previous consultation. But he rapidly became convinced
of its political merits, since it seemed to provide a means of getting
round the problem of giving the Germans a free hand in the field of
heavy industry without a perpetuation of discrimination against them.
Monnet's way of thinking appealed to Acheson, precisely because,
like the French, he combined concern about French recovery with
views looking to a permanent solution of the German problem in a
form that would both preclude future Franco-German hostilities and
make it unlikely that Germany could be drawn away from the West by
any Russian offer. Although the Plan was represented in the United
States as being supported by all good Europeans, it must be remembered that at first there were some doubts about the plan that American support for it could help resolve. In Germany both industry and
government were divided, and Konrad Adenauer's personal authority
was required to get it accepted.

President Truman himself expressed his approval as early as May 19;

[1] See William Diebold, *The Schuman Plan* (Praeger, 1959), pp. 30–45.
[2] E. C. Garwood, *Will Clayton: A Short Biography* (University of Texas Press,
1958), p. 33.

and Acheson and others made various statements giving the Plan the American blessing even after it had become evident that negotiations would have to proceed without British participation. It also secured immediate support from Paul Hoffman, who applauded its general features of expanding production and eliminating trade barriers as well as the implied termination of the policy of economic restrictions on Germany. Finally, he saw in it a contribution to European integration. Similar support came from Averell Harriman during the Foreign Aid hearings in Congress in June 1950.

In Congress itself there was fairly general support based on the view that Europe's strength would be enhanced by further economic integration and by the conciliation of France and Germany. The Plan would also, it was hoped, help to diminish the need for further American aid to Europe. Congress showed itself particularly interested in the decartelization proposals of the Plan, and this aspect was carefully watched by American opinion during the subsequent negotiations.

In Congress criticism of the British refusal to participate was very heated, and some members vainly suggested suspending all aid to Britain in order to indicate America's displeasure. The only wholly discordant note seems to have come from a few persons who thought that the Plan might eventually be exploited in favor of purely German interests.

In official circles the British attitude met with regret rather than with censure; it is not clear whether any attempt was made to influence the British attitude.[3] Occasionally the belief was expressed that more rapid progress could be made without Britain, particularly in view of the British commitment to socialist policies, and there were hopes that should the conservatives return to power Britain might cooperate more closely, if it did not participate in these new arrangements. Here, there may have been another echo of Monnet's position, since it seems quite clear that from this time forward he went ahead with the construction of "Little Europe" on the assumption that its own successes would inevitably lead in the end to Britain coming in.

Although the United States was not, of course, a formal participant in the negotiations, Americans took a considerable part (behind the scenes) in drafting the treaty. Monnet himself sought advice, largely on technical matters relating to the establishment of a large quasi-

[3] Diebold, *op. cit.*, p. 554.

federal market, and Americans encouraged the formation of a community, which should be as little restrictionist as possible. They were also concerned, in view of the need to get waivers from the General Agreement on Tariffs and Trade (GATT) and OEEC, that there should be no compromise with completely free trade in the products covered by the Plan. They insisted that high-cost Belgian coal and Italian steel should be dealt with by transitional provisions only and not given permanent preferential treatment. There was also some American work on the antitrust provisions of the treaty. On the institutional side, the United States contribution was largely an indirect one. The Community Court seems to have been a wholly European idea, but in the course of drafting the regulatory powers of the High Authority, there was some study of the United States Interstate Commerce Commission.

The primary channel for these negotiations was the American Embassy in Paris, where William Tomlinson acted as the liaison between Ambassador David Bruce and the Europeans conducting the negotiations. He was joined in this by some of the staff of General Henry Parkman, who was the head of the ECA mission to France.

The negotiations ran into difficulties, which were increased by the United States sponsorship of German rearmament, which came to a head in September 1950. The French insisted that the Schuman Plan negotiations must be concluded first. Otherwise there was a risk of reviving a powerful Germany without any form of control.

From November 1950 a very important role in the Schuman Plan was played by the United States High Commissioner in Germany, John McCloy, who helped to win over German critics. American officials working for him acted as go-betweens in the talks about the Plan, particularly as they affected decartelization and the deconcentration of German industry.[4] Robert Bowie, at that time General Counsel in the office of the U.S. High Commissioner, and himself an enthusiast for federalism, was a key figure. McCloy's policy was to get German industry successfully reorganized before the treaty came into force and to wind up the international authority for the Ruhr. On the other side, Robert Patterson, a former United States Secretary of War, was engaged, in his capacity as a lawyer, to press the interests of German

[4] *Ibid.*, pp. 554–56.

stockholders who were opposed to decartelization. McCloy and Adenauer eventually reached agreement in March 1951, and McCloy, as
well as the French and British High Commissioners, joined in pressing
for speedy ratification of the treaty.

Another American figure to be involved was George Ball, a lawyer
practicing in Washington whom Monnet invited to be the consultant to the French government on the development of the treaty,
and who publicly defended it, particularly in regard to its political
aspects, in the American press. The prestige of General Eisenhower
was also mobilized in support of the Plan. Finally, a tentative understanding was given that some financial aid would be made available to
the new authority.

The treaty itself was initialed on March 19, 1951, and the last ratification, that of Italy, was completed on June 16, 1952. The formal organization of the Coal and Steel Community was completed in September.

In the United States there was general approval of the move in labor quarters, though this was given conditionally on the new institutions acting effectively to prohibit cartels, and on German political development continuing in a democratic direction. Industry was perhaps
more divided. There was general concern that the Plan should not develop into a supercartel. The coal industry was generally favorable,
but Clarence B. Randall, the President of the Inland Steel Corporation, a former consultant on steel to ECA, attacked the Plan "as a sacrifice of industrial interests to political goals, as an embodiment of the
features of a cartel, as a limitation of free competition by means
which would be impermissible in the United States and as an avenue
to socialism." Other businessmen took a more favorable view, though
the United States was clearly obliged in their view to try to discourage
the Community from pursuing policies that might be detrimental to
American interests. It was of course desirable for the United States government to persuade the American taxpayer that funds were not being
used to finance the growth of heavy industry in Europe to a point at
which it might have an unfavorable impact on the United States itself.

In the more technical economic journals as well as in the public
press, comment was favorable, though, of course, some weaknesses
were seen. While Clarence Streit was critical of the Plan as a possible
impediment to wider schemes of unity, others supported it on the first-
step principle. Some people who saw the Plan in general as a gain for

American policy in Europe, since it made possible the French acceptance of German rearmament without a security guarantee, doubted
whether its economic effects would in fact live up to its political claims.
There were those finally, who questioned its consistency with America's professed concern for the unity of Germany. And for others, any
steps that looked like increasing the weight of Germany in Europe
were themselves regarded as dangerous.

It is undoubtedly true that the American support for the Plan did
mark a final breach with the wartime policies of restricting German
industry and the postwar policy of a separate international authority
for the Ruhr that would place German heavy industry under special
controls. American influence was used to persuade the French to
eliminate from the scheme anything that looked like a perpetuation of
such controls. The Coal and Steel Community was not to be a successor
to the international authority for the Ruhr, but rather a symbol of the
French willingness to accept Germany as a partner in the building up
of a supranational structure for Europe, and to permit the development of German industries for the benefit of Europe as a whole.
The Americans were clearly convinced by now that no policy that
looked to the long-term perpetuation of German weakness was to be
maintained.

In all these developments the role of the American Occupation Authorities in Germany was of the first importance. They were convinced
that the recovery of Europe could not be accomplished without a German contribution; the natural complementarity of German coal
and French iron ore offered a great opportunity for linking together
the two former enemies and overcoming the greatest single anomaly
that resulted from the organization of the European economy within
the limitations set by the existence of national frontiers. A minor point
was that some of those working in the field on the American side were
former German citizens, who may have been brought up to attach a
good deal of importance to the role of the Zollverein in the making of
German national unity in the nineteenth century. They were consequently susceptible to the basic thesis that political integration could
be achieved through economic means.

On the other side, it is probably again important to emphasize that
the Plan was launched before the Korean invasion, and before the Soviet military threat had become uppermost in Western European
thinking. What the French were interested in was international con-

trol to prevent German industry from being in a position to renew its pressure for an aggressive foreign policy. For nearly all concerned, the policy of Western integration seemed both more serious and more immediate than the problem of German unity.

The fortunes of the Coal and Steel Community need not be followed further, except to note that the American sympathy expressed at the beginning was reiterated on various occasions. In a statement in August 1952, Secretary Acheson said: "It is the intention of the United States to give the Coal and Steel Community the strong support that its importance to the political and economic unification of Europe warrants." The Mutual Security Act of 1952, approved on June 20, included an authorization for rendering assistance directly to the Community, though this provision was not made use of. David Bruce was accredited as Ambassador to the High Authority at Luxembourg in 1952 and held the post until 1955 when he was succeeded by W. Walton Butterworth who in 1958 was also accredited to the European Economic Community and EURATOM.

In 1952 it was announced that the United States would deal directly with the Coal and Steel Community on matters concerning coal and steel, and not with individual countries. In 1954, during a visit by Monnet to the United States in his capacity as President of the High Authority of the Community, he concluded a loan agreement for one hundred million dollars. From a strictly commercial point of view the loan was probably not necessary, but it helped to give status to the High Authority and so strengthened its position as against the member governments. The United States also assisted the Community in obtaining certain concessions under the GATT, and there was a modest reciprocal trade agreement between the United States and the Community in 1956.

Other proposals for economic integration under study by the OEEC in 1950, the Stikker, Pella, and Petsche plans,[5] do not seem to have attracted much American interest, though the first of these would have required American financing; and the ECA also lost its concern for other possible groupings on a subregional basis. Indeed, the accent in American thinking was now shifting rapidly from the economic to the military and political planes.

[5] William Adams Brown, Jr. and Redvers Opie, *American Foreign Assistance* (Brookings Institution, 1953) , pp. 294–300.

CHAPTER VI

Unity Within a European or Atlantic Framework?

IN ANSWER TO A QUESTION from a member of a subcommittee of the Senate Committee on Foreign Relations under Senator Theodore Green, which held hearings in Europe in July 1951, Milton Katz, then a special representative of the Economic Cooperation Administration (ECA) in Europe, said:

> . . . In February of this year we sent a letter to all of the participating countries of OEEC, in which we stated to them that from that time on we would no longer allocate aid on the old Marshall Plan basis, but that every judgment with respect to the allocation of aid from that point forward would be made in terms of defense support. It seems to me that for most practical purposes, therefore, Senator, the Marshall Plan as such has come to an end.

The reason for this fact lay, of course, in the interpretations placed on the outbreak of the Korean War, and in particular in the belief that a similar attempt to extend the Communist area of the world by force might be made in Western Europe. This belief was not limited to the Americans. The Europeans, and in particular the Germans, set up a clamor for greater military protection. In August 1950, Winston Churchill and Paul Reynaud had proposed a European army, rather vaguely defined, to the Council of Europe at Strasbourg. But it was only in response to the American pressure for immediate consent to German rearmament that Premier René Pleven produced on October 24, 1950, the germ of the plan that eventually led to the treaty for a European Defense Community (EDC). After the December 1950 meeting of the NATO Council it became clear that Britain would not participate in such a development, and when in February 1951 a conference started in Paris, it was confined to the six countries that had worked together on the Schuman Plan. The new Conservative Government in Britain, which took office in October 1951, did not shift its position on the main issue, although it expressed its sympathy with the efforts of the Six (France, Germany, Italy, Belgium, the Netherlands, and Luxembourg).

It is not surprising that people who had been involved in the earlier phase of European recovery wished to show that the new developments marked no departure in principle from what they had been doing. Paul Hoffman himself published a short book in 1951 under the title *Peace Can Be Won,* in which he said: "Obviously the greatest single contribution the ECA could make to Europe's enduring prosperity was to help it towards economic integration." Although Europe was still plagued by tariffs, the trend toward autarky had been reversed. In turn, it was the atmosphere of mutuality, exemplified in the European Payments Union, that had "made it possible for the Schuman Plan to be born." And the importance of the Schuman Plan and other advances on the economic front was to be found, he said, in "the impetus and inspiration they are giving to Western Europeans to duplicate in the political and in defense areas, the same kind of cooperation and integration that they are achieving in economic affairs."

In their pamphlet published in August that year, *Making Western Europe Defensible,* which has already been referred to,[1] Theodore Geiger and van Buren Cleveland summarized the economic argument in favor of European integration which had figured in their internal memoranda for the ECA. They now accepted the view that the position of Britain was quite different from that of its continental neighbors, and that what was needed now was a continental European union within an Atlantic framework. They asked why United States leadership, which had been so successful in the case of the Marshall Plan, had come up against obstacles in regard to rearmament, and declared that the reasons lay in American attempts to run counter to the convictions of the continental countries themselves. If the European countries remained separate, they would tend to become satellites of the United States, and a reaction to this position would drive them toward neutralism. The Pleven plan, on the other hand, represented the only rational way of dealing with the military problems of the continent, and was the only way of persuading the Germans themselves to take up the burden of armaments.

[1] Chapter 3, n. 13.

The role of the United States itself in the origins of the EDC negotiations and in their outcome will be dealt with, subsequently, but the immediate point to note is the relatively limited attention to the question of European economic integration in the public hearings on the Mutual Security Program, as foreign aid was renamed in 1951. This was partly due, perhaps, to the fact that no money was requested directly for promoting integration, and partly to the fact that Congress was fairly satisfied with the administration's efforts. Some further light on the general question can be got from the hearings before the special subcommittee already referred to. General Eisenhower, who had become a strong protagonist of integration from the military point of view, told the committee that he was very hopeful that many of the problems "would disappear if the whole area of Western Europe were one federal union." In reply to Senator Wiley, who asked him whether he saw any hope for a United States of Europe, Charles Spofford, the United States deputy representative on the NATO council, said:

> You say a united states of Europe, based on a counterpart of our United States? That is, a close federal union? I don't see any hope in that in the next few years. I see a very real sign of what General Eisenhower mentioned, an increasing feeling on the part of a great many Europeans, and what is more important, on the part of the youth of France and Germany, that the future of France and Germany depends on their getting together.

Spofford's evidence was echoed by Ambassador David Bruce, who said:

> There is a development going on in Europe which has been in progress for some time. . . . When I appeared before your committee about two years ago in Washington, a great many of your members were interested in this subject. At that time we had very little that we could say about it, because very little had transpired in this field. The subject is Western European integration, unification, federation, or whatever one wants to call it. In that, France has assumed a position of leadership.

In the upshot, Congress wrote into the act of October 19, 1951, as an objective of policy, the phrase the "economic unification and political integration of Europe."

During the summer of 1951 the State Department itself apparently came to believe that the political unification of Europe was something that the United States should encourage more actively, and at the meeting between representatives of Congress and the Council of Europe that autumn the Americans pressed quite hard in this direction.[2] It therefore looked at the end of the year as though the United States, while having no particular proposals in mind, was disposed to increase its pressure for unity.

The United States government welcomed the decision of the council of the Organization for European Economic Cooperation (OEEC) taken in March 1952 that the organization should continue to pursue its policies of promoting economic cooperation among its members even though the European Recovery Program itself was being wound up. But no new suggestions were offered on the American side. The Europeans discussed a possible common agricultural market, the so-called "Green Pool," and the European office of the Mutual Security Agency (MSA) declared that this "would be another step in uniting and strengthening the free peoples of Western Europe." A similar sympathy was expressed for the proposed extension of the pool concept to electric power. By this time, however, there were again considerable doubts in some American quarters about the compatibility of such concentration on Europe with the general American position in favor of universalism. As an example of such crosscurrents, the statement made by the American representatives at the Food and Agricultural Organization Conference in 1951 may be referred to. This attempted to combine a justification of the program of regional integration with the consistent support that the United States had shown for "international collaboration for the improvement of production and marketing, the reduction of trade barriers and the expansion of trade on a nondiscriminatory basis." In their view, "regional integration should be directed toward improving the efficiency of production and marketing, the progressive elimination of trade barriers and the expansion of trade, not only on a regional but also on a world-wide basis."

But by now political considerations were dominant. A Soviet note on March 19, 1952, had suggested a peace treaty that would restore to Germany within its existing frontiers its national unity and national army, provided that Germany did not join NATO. But at the same time the NATO Lisbon meeting set goals for Western defense that

[2] See Max Beloff, *Foreign Policy and the Democratic Process* (Johns Hopkins University Press, 1954) , pp. 100, 108–09.

made German participation absolutely necessary. And any ideas of "disengagement" in official circles were to disappear with the coming into office of the new administration on January 12, 1953.

It is not surprising that there was again not much discussion on European integration in the hearings on the 1952 Mutual Security Act.[3] There were very few doubts expressed on the wisdom of the integrationist policy or on whether the Europeans themselves wanted it. The act itself included an even more forthright statement than in past years:

> The Congress welcomes the recent progress in political federation, military integration and economic unification in Europe and reaffirms its belief in the necessity of further vigorous efforts toward these ends as a means of building strength, establishing security, and preserving peace in the North Atlantic area. In order to provide further encouragement to such efforts, the Congress believes it essential that this act should be so administered as to support concrete measures for political federation, military integration and economic unification in Europe.

The administration itself had proposed that the law should provide that funds could be used to assist any "organization, association or grouping of such [European] nations which in the opinion of the President makes a significant contribution towards political federation, military integration or economic unification of such nations." Congress, however, refused to give a blanket authority of this kind and restricted it to NATO, the Coal and Steel Community and the "organization which may evolve from current international discussions concerning a European Defense Community."

For most of the rest of 1952 the United States was occupied with a presidential election. The planks of both the parties were favorable to European unification, and no great difference between them can be detected.

Meanwhile, not much progress was being made within the larger Europe toward its common objectives of freer trade and general convertibility. The limitations on the power of the European Payments Union to fulfill the promise of economic integration or to solve the dollar problem were more widely recognized. Fears were expressed in the United States lest measures designed to improve the balance of pay-

---

[3] The act was approved on June 20, 1952.

ments of European countries might lead to discrimination against dollar goods. American and Canadian officials took part in preparing the 4th Annual Report of the OEEC, which expressed disappointment with the degree of liberalization achieved. And early in 1953, a publication of the Economic Commission for Europe (ECE) entitled "An Economic Survey of Europe since the War" also gave a pessimistic account of the progress made toward European economic integration.

The general level of political interest in the matter in the United States had not diminished much in 1952, but there remained the difficulty of distinguishing developments in Europe from those within the Atlantic framework. Senator Connally, who was one of the few public doubters about the wisdom of pressing for political unification in Europe, wrote: "The strengthening of the North Atlantic community, the promotion of European integration, the build-up of defense forces and the development of sound economic and social forces in Western Europe are so interrelated that many branches of our national government at home and abroad are involved, and our participation demands a common coordinated effort." He described the objectives of the President's special representative in Europe under the Mutual Security Program, Ambassador William H. Draper, as being one of "continuing efforts in cooperation with our European partners to support concrete measures for political federation, military integration and economic unification."

He further wrote that progress toward economic integration was "a most encouraging development. It is only by means of furthering and encouraging this development that we can hope to see Europe strong enough eventually to stand on her own feet. To permit integration in the military and economic fields to become effective, there must be, I believe, some kind of political federation which should of course be shaped by the Europeans themselves." [4]

The reference in general terms to an Atlantic community, in the Truman-Churchill communiqué of January 9, 1952, had led to some discussions whether the economic arrangements of the European countries should be broadened out onto an Atlantic basis.[5] But in the

[4] Senator Tom Connally, *Report on Western Europe*, 82 Cong., 2 sess. (1952).

[5] The problem of the relations between "European Union" and "Atlantic Union" is discussed in the concluding chapter of M. M. Ball, *N.A.T.O. and the European Union Movement* (London, 1959).

economic field the American government was very little disposed to look at Atlantic arrangements. The United States opposed the British attempt made at this time to reduce the functions of the OEEC and to transfer them to NATO, in part on the grounds that the OEEC was an organization for fostering economic integration in Europe, which was itself a policy of the United States. It was pointed out that one of the objectives of this policy had been to reduce rather than to increase the formal governmental ties between the United States and Europe.

On the military production side some indirect impetus was given to European integration by NATO. For although the United States made little use of European facilities for producing military supplies for the American armed forces, it placed orders in some European countries for deliveries to others, thus forcing them to undertake some coordination of military production.

There was little indication that the United States would in fact accept any broadening of the European institutions to include the North American countries. But some thinking in economic quarters did proceed and this culminated in the so-called "Green Book," produced within the Mutual Security Agency. The proposals made in this document were undoubtedly unpalatable to the Treasury, which was still opposed to measures on an Atlantic basis because of its desire to return to the fully convertible currencies and world trading order of the pre-1914 era.[6]

The "Green Book" proposals would have involved setting up a multi-billion dollar stabilization fund, to be called the Atlantic Reserve System, as well as an Atlantic Economic Board to coordinate trade and other policies affecting currency relationships. An Atlantic Commodity Board, subordinated to the Economic Board, would have sought to stabilize production and prices of essential raw materials through long-term agreements with leading producer countries, and thereby to remove the need for restrictive cartel arrangements: "By tying together the major currency systems of the Atlantic community, the dollar and the pound sterling, and another unit expected to evolve from the six-member European Defense Community, the new approach, those who take it hope, would end the preoccupation abroad

---

[6] The "Green Book" is still classified. The summary that follows, whose accuracy I have no reason to doubt, is based on the report by Felix Belair, *New York Times,* Oct. 29, 1952.

with dwindling gold reserves that has prevented expansionist economic policies." The objections of the Treasury, it was suggested, lay in the fact that the reserve pool for such a system would have very largely to come from the United States, and also because it would duplicate functions already in the hands of the International Monetary Fund: "It is argued that with all the free nations hard put to it to finance their rearmament goals, while maintaining living standards and coping with dollar deficits, the Reserve Fund would soon be used for purposes that should properly be covered by private or intergovernmental loans or grants in aid."

It was noted that the membership in both the Reserve System and the Economic Board would be limited at the outset to the United States and Great Britain, with only ultimate provision for a representative of the projected European community and that this might indicate a belief on the part of the authors of this document that this could be held out as a further incentive for the rapid creation of such a community.

It was rapidly made clear that the "Green Book" did not represent official American policy, and that the majority view was that nothing short of a universalist approach would meet the problems of the current period. But in this perspective Western Europe itself might seem to be only a makeshift grouping as far as trade and payments were concerned. A view along these lines was put forward in a general survey of what had been done in the field of economic cooperation between 1947 and 1952 by an author who had had exceptional opportunities for observing the development of American policy.

> The principal economic justification for pressing for further cooperation confined to Western Europe would be a pragmatic one: the ability to secure removal of more trade and payments barriers within the group than among a larger number of countries without impairing Western Europe's ability to earn its way in world trade. As we have seen, in the postwar period there has been more action to remove trade barriers among the OEEC countries than among any of the members of the larger groupings, but the results still fall far short of creating the single market sought by proponents of Western European integration.
>
> Western European economic integration cannot reasonably be the primary goal of economic policy, either for the countries of the area or for the United States. The British government's persistent

refusal to subordinate its overseas economic relations to those with Western Europe has been accentuated by Britain's greater interest than most Continental countries in overseas trade, and complicated by the policies of economic control—and perhaps also by the prejudices—of the Labour Government. But even if sometimes exaggerated, British policy embodies an understanding of the duality of trading interests—in Western European cooperation and in global, or non-Soviet, cooperation—which all the OEEC countries have in some degree. The difference between the British and, say, the French view as to how much emphasis to put on one or the other area of cooperation, and the disagreement whether one conflicted with the other, have reflected political considerations as well as economic analysis. No flat statements would do justice to either case. Now the new concentration on rearmament, and the growing importance of the North Atlantic Treaty Organization, embodying most of the OEEC countries but not limited to them, have—like Secretary Marshall's initiative in 1947—once again altered the setting in which the possibilities and implications of Western European cooperation must be judged.[7]

So far we have been concentrating on official and congressional opinion. At some point note must be taken of the fact that general public opinion in the United States was also involved. But at the same time, one must be aware that one is here entering on a particularly difficult aspect of the subject, since the importance of pressure groups and other instruments in the field of public opinion is especially difficult to assess where the field of foreign affairs is concerned. It may be possible to trace the acts of particular individuals or organizations, but these may in the long run seem less important than the general bias of opinion. And in the particular case with which we are concerned the general sympathy of Americans for the idea of European unity is probably more significant than anything else. Nevertheless, one cannot ignore the fact that attempts were made to capitalize on this sentiment for action both within the United States and even in Europe itself.[8]

It was early realized by the European adherents of the movement for integration that wide American support would be necessary, and in

[7] William Diebold, *Trade and Payments in Western Europe* (Harper, 1952), pp. 416–17.
[8] The following paragraphs are based in part on the important piece of research undertaken by my pupil, M. F-X. Rebattet, a French student of St. Antony's College, Oxford, for his unpublished thesis: "The European Movement (1945–1953)."

November 1946 and again in July 1948 there were visits to the United States by the Secretary-General of the European Movement, Dr. Retinger, and Duncan Sandys, who at that time was a prominent figure in it. They succeeded in forming the nucleus of a committee of American sympathizers, including Allen Dulles and Senators J. W. Fulbright and Walter F. George. The "American Committee on United Europe," was actually launched during a luncheon given in honor of Winston Churchill. It took another year, however, to establish it on a permanent footing. Its purposes included not only publicity for the movement in the United States, but also the collection of money to help finance the movement in Europe.

In its statement of purposes it was declared that the committee had been formed "by a group of private American citizens" who felt "that organized unofficial support for the ideal of European unity" might prove to be "the determining factor in the direction that Europe will take during the second half of the twentieth century." It is obvious that the motive for many of those who gave their support to the committee was very directly related to the cold war and the threat of communism.

The difficulty of distinguishing between unity on a European basis and on an Atlantic one confronted the public pressure groups as it had the policy makers. And in 1951 an attempt was made by the American Committee to sign a joint statement with the Atlantic Union Committee. This had been proposed by the latter and would have stressed European Union as a first step toward Atlantic union. "The American Committee on United Europe" submitted the proposal to the European Movement itself, which rejected it, and the rejection was acquiesced in by the American Committee. In the committee as finally set up businessmen predominated, but there were a number of distinguished members of Congress from both houses. The names of its Chairman, General William Donovan, and its Vice-Chairman, Allen Dulles, suggested a close connection with American official circles, particularly on the intelligence side.

The committee did not aim at a mass membership. It numbered by 1951 only about one hundred persons, nor did it attempt much in the way of coordination of propaganda, though it did sponsor lecture tours by prominent Europeans including Jean Monnet, Paul-Henri Spaak, Winston Churchill and Paul Reynaud. On the lecture tour by

Spaak, the *New York Times* commented on February 27, 1951: "One of the more striking proofs that the United States has come of age is the interest being taken here in the movement for European unity. That some very distinguished American citizens should be giving their time and money to promoting a movement in which we have no immediate stake or prospect of gain is evidence that our role as the leading democracy is being taken seriously." Senator Vandenberg was quoted in a document circulated by the committee as follows: "It is a somewhat delicate matter for American citizens to recommend political and economic reforms to the citizens of other nations without being misunderstood both at home and abroad. But we all have a common denominator of mutual interest in the objectives which the committee would sustain."

The committee early revealed the direction of its own thinking. On December 20, 1949, General Donovan wrote to various European statesmen, stressing the committee's doubts about the performance of the Council of Europe at its first session, and pointing out that little progress had been made toward creating a European political authority. The replies were released in time for the Senate hearings on the 1950 Marshall Plan appropriations, and proved helpful despite the conflicting approaches between the statesmen of the Six and the rest. Donovan himself testified before the House Committee on March 3, 1950: "I believe that we have a stake in Western Europe, one that we must not risk losing because we must wage and win the war in which we now find ourselves, none the less dangerous because it is a subversive and not a shooting war. That is why I believe in the necessity of a united Europe."

In line with this it may be noted that when Dr. Retinger asked Sandys to resign his position on March 21, 1950, he gave as a reason not only that the various movements composing the European Movement were looking with increasing suspicion on his activities, but also that their American friends did not agree with his tactics.

In the publications of the American Committee the word "integration" began to replace "United" Europe and European "Union." A message of support to Schuman on his plan for a Coal and Steel Community was released on June 19, 1950, with a powerful set of signatories including General Marshall, Henry L. Stimson, and Chester Bowles. This message also included criticism of the British unwillingness to participate: "In taking this insular position the British Labour Party is not speaking for the Socialist parties in Europe." Britain, it prophesied, would however come round to a more constructive viewpoint.

By far the most important work of the American Committee was on the money-raising side. The lecture tours it sponsored were largely motivated by the hope of raising money from the business community, particularly since contributions to the committee had been declared tax-deductible. But an important fraction of its funds undoubtedly came from official sources. With the money available the American Committee helped both the European Movement in general, and particular aspects of it such as the European Youth Campaign. It was the American Committee also that financed the Action Committee for a European Supra-National Community which was responsible for organizing the whole campaign for the EDC. But this financial aid was naturally enough kept in the background, since it would have provided an obvious weapon of hostile propaganda for the left-wing opponents of the European integration movement. Assistance from the Americans was also forthcoming on the intellectual side. When, on March 6, 1952, Spaak set up a "study commission" for a European constitution, Robert Bowie and Professor Carl Friedrich of Harvard were associated with their work.[9]

The European movement's journal was almost completely financed by subscriptions from the Mutual Security Agency and from the American Committee, and when these stopped in 1954, it had to cease publication. The Treasurer of the movement in 1953 asked its National Councils to provide more money, since it was not desirable that American money should be used for the ordinary running costs of the movement. But in fact the National Councils had also made calls on American funds, notably those of France and Italy.

After the failure of the EDC, the American Committee on United Europe became less important, but it survived until November 1960. A statement made at that time by the chairman of its board of directors explained its demise as follows: "Recent far-reaching progress towards European unification and wide popular support achieved for integration in Europe has resulted in a decision by the American Committee on United Europe to suspend its major activities." But a hint

[9] See R. R. Bowie and C. J. Friedrich (eds.), *Studies in Federalism* (Little, 1954).

was given that new tasks might demand the resuscitation of the committee, and a further element of Atlantic-European ambiguity was provided by the statement that the logical successor and heir of the committee was the recently established Atlantic Institute.

One reason the committee's activities had become less important was the establishment in Washington in June 1954 of an office for the European Coal and Steel Community. Monnet had set up this office when the failure of the EDC became probable, and when he felt that it was important to convince American opinion that the European idea would survive this setback and in particular that the Coal and Steel Community would continue in being. The office later took over the representation of both the European Economic Community and EURATOM.

But this is to anticipate. It is now necessary to go back and trace the American relationship to the second major attempt at integration in Little Europe, namely the European Defense Community.

CHAPTER VII

The United States and the Defense of Europe

WRITING IN 1954 an American student said: "The foreign policy of the United States since 1949, of both the Truman and Eisenhower administrations, has rested on the rearmament of the Germans inside the EDC. This establishes an essential tie between continental European union and U.S. foreign policy." [1] The issue was never quite as simple as that, since some of the protagonists of European union deplored the fact that it had got itself tangled up with the stormier issue of German rearmament. The idea of a European army, though publicly voiced only after the beginning of the Korean War, was not a new one for the Americans. There had been talk of one as early as 1946, partly in relation to what should be done with the Poles and Czechs in the armed forces of the Western Allies, who were unwilling to return to their countries of origin. It was obvious that something of this kind might be the way to overcome European objections to the rearmament of Germany, and suggestions along these lines came from the American High Commission in Germany as early as July 1950.

The Pleven Plan, which was the French reply to the American proposal for German rearmament, was produced with such speed that it looks as though the French had been working on it for some time. Their original scheme was for the international integration to take place at the regimental level, that is to say, the largest national units were to be battalions. The plan was not of course acceptable to American military thinking, and the United States prevailed on Britain and

---

[1] F. S. C. Northrop, *European Union and United States Foreign Policy: A Study in Sociological Jurisprudence* (Macmillan, 1954), p. 13.

France to accept a policy of including German contingents directly within the NATO structure.

Two sets of negotiations were now proceeding simultaneously, those for the restoration of German sovereignty and those for a measure of German rearmament. It had not been foreseen that the Germans would prove relatively unwilling to rearm, and that they would make the provision of troops conditional on meeting their demands in the matter of national sovereignty. This was the position taken by Adenauer at the beginning of 1951. What the Germans wanted if they were to rearm was a national army and general staff and a full complement of war industries.

General Eisenhower's visit to Europe in January 1951 convinced him that the Germans would not accept less than this, and that the only alternative was to go back to the idea of a European army, a view which also commended itself to the American High Commission. The proposals of the Americans as well as those of the French put forward in March still assumed an unequal status for the Germans. But in June 1951 the French position was reversed and the idea of equality accepted. Talks on the new basis began in June.

The Americans, probably overestimating the speed at which German contingents could be raised, now set themselves to persuade the Germans to agree to the new formulation. And they took an active part behind the scenes in the long drawn out negotiations which transformed the Pleven Plan into a treaty for a European Defense Community (EDC) signed on May 27, 1952. This was done partly by linking the negotiations to the working out of a "contractual agreement" in place of the Occupation Statute, so as to restore to the German authorities control over all their internal affairs, and the major part of their foreign policy as well, except where it related to the occupation agreements with the Russians. After the failure of the renewed bout of negotiations with the Russians at the "Palais Rose" talks in Paris from March to June 1951, this exception seemed relatively less important, since the newly sovereign German government would be likely at any rate for some considerable time to align its policies with those of the United States.

It is fairly clear that General Eisenhower himself was one of the foremost influences in bringing about the rather radical change in the

American attitude. He made his point of view public in a widely reported speech to the English Speaking Union at the London Guildhall
on July 3, 1951, in which he said: "It would be difficult to overstate
the benefit, in these years of stress and tension, that would accrue to
NATO if the free nations of Europe were truly a unit." He himself
was almost certainly convinced from his wartime experience of the
feasibility of a multinational force of this kind, and while the United
States had officially to make it clear to the recalcitrant Europeans that
the adoption of the scheme would not bring about a withdrawal of
American forces from Europe, Eisenhower himself seems to have hoped
that in the not too distant future this might indeed be possible. Speaking to Senator Green's Subcommittee, General Alfred Gruenther said:
"General Eisenhower's contention here is that Western Europe must
be able to defend itself." He went on to express his view that American
ground forces should not be kept in foreign countries over a long period of years. On the question of a European Army, General Gruenther said: "General Eisenhower has not been into the European army
matter yet. We find that this is what is happening. The European nations, who are having some problems in connection with this, feel that
General Eisenhower should be in on that. So beginning Monday [23
July 1951] we are going to participate as an observer in these European Army discussions."

Eisenhower himself told the committee that he had been much encouraged by the evidence of greater closeness between Germany and
France:

> I believe in it this much—when I came over here I disliked the
> whole idea of a European Army and I had enough troubles without
> it. However, I have decided that it offers another chance for bringing
> another link in here, so I made up my mind to go into the thing
> with both feet . . . So I am going to try to help, and I realize that a
> lot of my professional associates are going to think I am crazy. But
> I am going to tell you that joining Europe together is the key to the
> whole thing.

The political advantages of the scheme were similarly expounded by
Ambassador David Bruce in the same hearings. Most importantly,
from the American standpoint, he said, it would mean this: "I assume
that all of us some day would like to see the withdrawal from the continent of as large a number of our forces as possible, if not in their

totality." And this the EDC would help to bring about. Meanwhile the conclusion of such a treaty would help to preclude any possibility of Western Germany swinging eastwards—a development which would leave the Americans "faced with a most unenviable situation."

"In the whole history of modern civilization in Europe," said Bruce, "no steps have ever been taken so remarkable, so revolutionary, as those which have been taken and reached the point where they have now arrived, towards the formulation of what it is hoped on the part of those most interested in them will become a true federation of Europe." This goal had not been attainable through the alternative route of NATO because the British were unwilling to surrender more of their sovereignty than the United States was prepared to do.

Similar sentiments were echoed by Secretary Dean Acheson in his speech at the time of the signature of the treaty on May 27, 1952, when he said, "We have seen the beginning of the realization of an ancient dream—the unity of the free peoples of Western Europe." And the concrete nature of the American support for the plan was demonstrated in the Mutual Security Act of 1952, when it was provided, as we have seen, that part of the funds should go directly to the European Defense Community when it came into being.

For the next two years, however, the question in Europe was to be whether the treaty itself could be ratified, and in particular by the French. In this part of the story the United States was very active indeed: "Washington having cold-shouldered the Pleven proposal later shifted to the opposite extreme and came to look upon the EDC as the cornerstone of America's foreign policy." [2]

In order to understand this period of American policy, notice must be taken of the fact that when in January 1953 General Eisenhower himself succeeded Harry Truman as President of the United States, his new Secretary of State was John Foster Dulles. Dulles in turn called in as head of the Policy Planning Staff Professor Robert R. Bowie, who was, as we have seen, unlike his predecessor under Acheson, Paul Nitze, an enthusiast for European integration.

For even though it could be argued that the policy was basically un-

[2] Michael T. Florinsky, *Integrated Europe?* (Macmillan, 1955), p. 104. For the subsequent fortunes of the treaty and the arguments relating to it, see especially Chapter 4, "European Union: Setback and Revival," in B. T. Moore, *NATO and the Future of Europe* (Harper, 1958).

changed between the two administrations, since Acheson himself had argued that Europe would attract America by its unity but repel it by disunity, the new impetus imparted by Dulles's personality should not be discounted. Dulles himself had been a close friend of Jean Monnet since the Paris Peace Conference of 1919 and had been associated with him in business in the interwar years. According to two well-informed observers, Monnet was indeed "his closest foreign friend." [3]

Dulles himself had never questioned since the war the desirability in general of some form of European unity, or the propriety of the United States exerting itself to bring it about. In a speech as early as February 10, 1947, he said "Of course increased unity depends primarily upon the continental peoples themselves. But the United States has there both moral rights and political power. Formerly, Europe could have its wars without involving us. Now American blood, shed in two European wars, gives us the moral right to speak." Furthermore, the position of the United States in Germany gave it a special claim to be heard, for "what is done with that power will either promote unity in Europe or perpetuate disunity. We have a responsibility that is inescapable." The important thing was to make continental Europe something better than the "rickety fire-hazard of the past." Dulles had also been with Marshall in Europe during the Marshall Plan period and had discussed the problem of the Ruhr with French leaders, including Charles de Gaulle and Leon Blum. He seems to have been one of the first to have thought of an international solution for the Ruhr industries as an alternative to the prolongation of control by the occupying powers.

If the Soviet Union would not cooperate in advancing continental unity as a whole, a worthwhile start could still be made in Western Europe. In his book *War or Peace*, published in 1950, Dulles had again shown himself much concerned over the problem. In this book NATO is treated as a regional association alongside the Rio Pact of September 2, 1947. The Marshall Plan is discussed under the head of "Filling in the Economic Vacuum in Europe," while the Brussels Pact appears in "Filling in the Political Vacuum."

[3] Roscoe Drummond and Gaston Coblentz, *Dual at the Brink* (Doubleday, 1960), p. 18. The same authors point out that Dulles was the first Secretary of State whose continental links (with Monnet and Chancellor Adenauer) were closer than his British ones, and that he was therefore less affected than Acheson by the British inhibitions over a close-knit Europe.

He pointed out that until 1949 it had not been worthwhile in most people's view to try to fill in the military vacuum because of the protection of the American nuclear weapon. But Europeans had made the point that the knowledge that an attack on them would bring about a general war in which the United States would eventually emerge as victor was inadequate. For such a victory would come too late to prevent the destruction of civilization in Western Europe. For these reasons Dulles had insisted during his short period in the Senate that the Military Assistance Program should be closely tied to the North Atlantic Treaty.[4] Dulles had been close to Eisenhower in the 1952 campaign and looked at the question very much in the same way. The EDC was primarily a way of getting the Europeans to accept a proper share of the burden of the common defense. But it was also a guarantee of Europe developing along the general lines that Dulles favored. He increasingly identified his own prestige with the ratification of the treaty, despite warnings from some quarters that the probabilities were that it would not pass and despite some feeling that the pressure on the European governments, in particular on the French, might harm the treaty's prospects.

In the United States, particularly in Congress, the support for Dulles' policy was widespread. An amendment to the Mutual Security Bill of 1953 which was accepted empowered the President to withhold up to $1 billion until such time as the EDC came into effect. In its report on the bill the Senate Committee on Foreign Relations said that the American Congress had in the past five years repeatedly expressed its interest in and approval of European integration, and declared it to be the wish of the committee to reaffirm the strong statement of the 1952 Mutual Security Act to this effect. In particular, the report went on, "the committee wishes to record its deep interest in the ratification of the European Defense Community Treaty." [5]

It has been suggested that Dulles was handicapped in Europe by the apparent commitment of the new administration to a policy of "libera-

[4] Dulles was nominated to the Senate in July 1949 on the resignation of Senator R. S. Wagner, but was defeated at the mid-term election in the following autumn. He subsequently served as Special Consultant to the State Department, but was then primarily concerned with the Japanese Peace Treaty. There is a general discussion of Dulles, perhaps rather underemphasizing his role as a protagonist of European unity, in Richard Goold-Adams, *The Time of Power* (London, 1962).

[5] *The Mutual Security Act of 1953*, S. Rept. 403, 83 Cong., 1 sess., p. 17.

tion" in Eastern Europe in place of the previous administration's policy of "containment," and that this inevitably led to a growth of neutralism and anti-Americanism which hampered his task. It has been argued, too, that a more flexible policy taking into account problems outside Europe could have been more effective in that concessions to France over Indo-China could have been made conditional on the ratification of the EDC, but that this could only have been done if Dulles were prepared to return to a position of "containment" which he in fact did return to, though too late to save the treaty.[6]

Throughout 1953 Dulles refused to consider possible alternatives to the EDC, and on December 14 he made his celebrated speech, talking of the necessity of an "agonizing reappraisal" of American policy in Europe if France were to reject the EDC Treaty. It has been pointed out that this attitude produced an impasse: "On this side of the Atlantic, it appeared on occasion that the distrust of some French circles for the means had blinded them to the continuing importance of the aims. On the other side of the Atlantic, it sometimes appeared that the concern of some American circles over the aims had caused an unduly rigid attachment to a specific means." [7]

It has been said that during the early part of 1954 Dulles was warned that the French would not ratify, but instructed his ambassadors in Europe not only to refuse to discuss possible alternative schemes but not even to admit that such alternatives existed.[8] The result was that when the French did reject the treaty in August, Dulles was quite unprepared to promote an alternative and at the same time clearly was unable to make good his implied threats that American assistance would be withdrawn from Europe. He was also very grudging in his attitude toward the initiative taken by Eden in September to provide a substitute for the EDC on the grounds that the Brussels Treaty, which it was proposed to expand for the purpose, was not a supranational document. In the end, however, he accepted the British scheme and Western European union duly came into being.[9] But this defeat af-

[6] This argument is expounded at some length by Northrop in *European Union and United States Foreign Policy*, Chapter 10.

[7] See the contribution by Milton Katz, "The Community of Europe and American Policy," in H. Field Haviland, Jr. (ed.), *The United States and the Western Community* (Haverford College Press, 1957), p. 11.

[8] Drummond and Coblentz, *op. cit.*, p. 85.

[9] See Sir Anthony Eden's memoirs, *Full Circle* (London, 1961), pp. 158–68.

fected both Dulles' view of the possible role of America in Europe and
the subsequent behavior of the American government, which became
much more circumspect.

This episode was an unhappy one in the history of Anglo-American
relations in Europe. Dulles may have been affected by France's suspicions of British attitudes toward European integration, since the nature of the Conservative's criticism of the Labour Government's unwillingness to take part in the Schuman Plan negotiations had suggested
that they really wished the British to take part in order to prevent
the scheme reaching fruition. On the military side the French were
still unwilling to go into a close relationship with the Germans without the British taking part. Some Americans believed that this fact
would have enabled Eden to have saved the EDC by making the kind
of proposals that he put forward after the breakdown, and that his
holding them up was due to a deliberate intention that the EDC
should not come into being. By no means all Americans agreed with
this view, but it was undoubtedly held in some quarters, and helps to
explain why, from about 1955, there was a general assumption within
the American administration that Britain's conduct in recent years
made it possible to unify Europe only if the British were excluded.
The gain in French self-confidence with the country's economic recovery from about 1956 brought something of an alignment on this point
between themselves and the Americans. It is noticeable that in the
late 1950's the British role in Europe was much less prominent than in
the preceding years.

In the quiet period after the storm over the EDC, it was natural for
Americans to look back and see where the policies they had pursued
over the decade since the end of the war had now brought them. A
rather skeptical inquiry was that of the historian M. T. Florinsky.
Florinsky took the view that the postwar movement for European integration was primarily a reaction to the Communist menace, though
some of its protagonists, like Monnet, believed in it for its own sake
irrespective of Soviet intentions. He also took the view that pressure
from English-speaking countries was more likely to damage than to
advance the cause: "American pressure was, indeed, a major factor behind the postwar move towards the unification of Europe but although
Washington realized that the implementation of this program would

encounter major difficulties, their magnitude and nature were not fully grasped." [10]

Florinsky did not deny that the Americans were concerned with the future of Europe. The question was, whether their strategy in this respect was a correct one:

> The political and military rehabilitation of Europe and the creation of a military alliance for the defense of the West are what may be deliberately termed the legitimate objectives of American policy essential to the well-being and security of the United States. How these objectives are achieved is a matter of secondary importance. If this argument is valid, it will appear that the concept of European integration, hurriedly devised by a few European enthusiasts and taken much too seriously on the banks of the Potomac, is but an exotic graft on the main body of American policy.[11]

A more favorable assessment was that contained in the report of a committee under the chairmanship of William Y. Elliott, which included a number of persons who had been active in pursuing the integrationist line from within government service.[12] A principal conclusion of this report was that the United States had developed since 1947 a more realistic appreciation of the shift in the political situation and of the impact of the war in Europe. It had also accepted the fact that its position in international economic discussions must be determined by its general foreign policy. And it was for this reason that the integration of Western Europe had become an acceptable objective:

> American policy since 1947 has included one major objective—the political and economic unification of Western Europe—which is clearly premised on the conclusion that, for this group of countries, even the continuous coordination of national policies through intergovernmental organizations like the OEEC and the EPU is insufficient, and that a formal merging or joint exercise of their national sovereignties is necessary if they are to achieve economic and political health and play their proper part in Western defense. American sponsorship of European Union has thus involved a quite basic qualification of the internationalist assumption that the nation-state system is adequate and immutable.[13]

[10] M. T. Florinsky, *Integrated Europe?* (Macmillan, 1955) , p. 28.
[11] *Ibid.*, p. 143.
[12] *The Political Economy of American Foreign Policy: Its Concepts, Strategy and Limits,* Report of a Study Group sponsored by the Woodrow Wilson Foundation and the National Planning Association (Henry Holt, 1955) .
[13] *Ibid.*, p. 216.

Although the authors of the report were generally favorable to the development of cooperation on an Atlantic basis, they accepted the view that the breakdown of confidence in the nation-state was confined to western continental Europe and was not present in either the United States or the United Kingdom. They therefore expressed the hope that the European countries which had combined in the Coal and Steel Community would go forward to a closer economic union, and were optimistic about the economic results. But these would demand a further measure of American support: "Throughout the preceding discussion the crucial dependence of these groupings on American political and economic support has been indicated. The survival of the Sterling Area, the conception and creation of the EPU, and the progress made towards European Union has depended directly on American leadership and American economic support." [14] The group made precise suggestions for American policy, notably in the fields of tariff reduction and of maintaining a high level of domestic demand, while on the institutional side they prophetically looked forward to the inclusion of the United States and Canada in a reshaped OEEC.

The principal point in the view of the authors was that advance on the Atlantic and the European fronts had to be undertaken simultaneously:

> It is noteworthy that these two principles of Western unification are complementary and interdependent. The progressive organization of the West depends on the exercise of American economic and political power. But if that power is to be acceptable to the European nations—if it is to be leadership rather than domination—it must be counter-balanced by strengthening the institutions of European unity and creating—and as soon as possible—a supranational European union. Conversely, European unification depends upon progress in the unification of the Atlantic community as a whole. [15]

Many of the themes explored in this discussion came up again in a symposium held in 1956 at Haverford College. [16] Here there were some skeptical voices. It was pointed out, for instance, that if the Six were to achieve an economic union—and by this time, of course, negotia-

[14] *Ibid.*, p. 288.
[15] *Ibid.*, p. 324.
[16] H. Field Haviland, Jr. (ed.), *The United States and the Western Community.*

tions for what became the Treaty of Rome were already in progress—this would increase their weight in the general international economy. The question was what they would do with it. "As long as they were little and weak," said Raymond Vernon, "there were compelling forces which required them to throw in what strength they had with the United States. Once they are merged, those forces change. How do you ensure that the forces of cohesion will be operated on your side and not on the other side?" [17]

But the main issue raised was once again that of Germany. Milton Katz, a former ECA official, pointed out that if the current deadlock persisted segments of German opinion might come to regard German adherence to the West as antithetical to German unification. A notion might emerge that Germany should be separated from NATO and the partnership of free Europe in order to make German unification possible. "In terms of American purposes and the purposes of the NATO partners, this would invert ends and means." On the other hand, Lincoln Gordon advanced the hypothesis "that it would be to the interests of the United States, as well as Germany, to have Germany unified but neutral, as Sweden is, rather than divided with the Western part allied with us." And he added that every time someone else in the community (in the group of the Six) or in the United States made a speech saying that the community was a wonderful idea because it would help make Western Germany forget its preoccupation with unification, this added fuel to the conviction in Western Germany that there was a definite collision between the two objectives.[18]

There were, of course, in addition those who recognized that the American policy had as one of its inevitable effects a commitment to keeping the CDU party in power in Germany, since the Socialists were believed to be unsound in this respect. There were indeed certain German voices which expressed themselves in this sense, and it was understandable that there should be some anxiety lest an expression of American interest in forwarding a particular foreign policy should

[17] *Ibid.*, p. 114.
[18] *Ibid.*, pp. 14–15, 98, 111. In 1952–54, the belief that the two objectives were not incompatible was still sincerely held by American policy makers. The basic difficulty was clearly revealed, however, in the exchanges with the Russians at the Foreign Ministers' Meeting, October–November 1955. George Kennan was among the few who remained fully alive to this problem. See Chapter 3 of his *Russia, The Atom and the West* (Harper, 1958) and his article "Disengagement Revisited," *Foreign Affairs* (January 1959).

overflow into apparent intervention in countries' domestic political controversies. Indeed, fears of this kind had been voiced throughout the Marshall Plan period.[19] But in general the argument was often restated at this time in familiar terms and even the view that the United States itself was an acceptable model for Europe found its advocates.[20] But such discussion in the mid-1950s mostly took place away from the general political arena. Once the period of massive economic aid was over, Congress itself abandoned much of its interest in European affairs and did not renew it until anxieties about trade and balance-of-payments questions began to be felt in 1958. It was jealous of calls on its time for external purposes, and rejected approaches from the Council of Europe for a further meeting between congressmen and the Council such as had produced the debate at Strasbourg in 1951 already referred to. Such interest as was shown by individual congressmen was usually the product of outside pressure, for instance from that indefatigable protagonist of Atlantic Union, Clarence Streit. There was perhaps a background awareness of the need for anchoring Germany solidly to the West, but not much concern about the details of how this was to be done.

[19] On the question of Germany, see also the chapter by Gordon Craig, in Klaus Knorr (ed.), *NATO and American Security* (Princeton University Press, 1959).

[20] See, for instance, the chapter by H. S. Commager, "The United States and the Integration of Europe," in C. G. Haines (ed.), *European Integration* (Johns Hopkins Press, 1957).

CHAPTER VIII

Europe's Changed Outlook
Economics and Strategy

WHILE PUBLIC DISCUSSION WAS PROCEEDING in the United States on familiar lines, the situation in Europe was a rapidly changing one. Most important perhaps was the change in the general strategic situation. In the spring of 1953, the United States had adopted a new military policy, stressing the role of the nuclear deterrent but at the same time accepting the likelihood of an indefinite prolongation of the cold war. The Americans were afraid that the arms race might overstrain the economy and took the view that a policy resting predominantly on nuclear weapons was the cheaper one. They also assumed that their own superiority in this respect would be maintained. On land, some "conventional" forces were required, and this meant helping to build up the armies of America's allies, while in view of the range of aircraft at the time, much importance was also attached to the acquisition of overseas bases.

After the failure to use the nuclear threat to bring about a more satisfactory conclusion of the war in Indo-China, and with the evidence that the Soviet Union was moving toward nuclear parity, policy began to shift once more, and the possibility of limited wars received a new exploration. Argument now revolved around the vulnerability of the deterrent bases and the future role of ballistic missiles. For the first time, the question had to be explored whether the NATO alliance was sufficient for the purposes which its makers had had in mind. In other words, if the United States itself was vulnerable to a nuclear attack, then the existence of an American guarantee was not a credible answer to some form of aggression on a lesser scale, even though it might still be sufficient to prevent a nuclear attack on Western Europe. The period between 1955 and 1961 was thus one which saw considerable divisions of opinion over strategical questions, enhanced by interservice controversies in the United States itself. It also saw important divergences between the United States and some of its European allies, notably France, and, with the growing economic strength of Western Europe, an increasing sensitivity on the part of Americans to the apparent unwillingness of Europeans to contribute an adequate proportion of the increment to the common defense.

Topics such as these belong more properly to the study of Western alliance as a whole and on them there exists a considerable literature.[1] But even if we try to restrict ourselves to Europe, where the new developments were primarily economic, it is essential to keep in mind this background of strategic and consequently of political uncertainty. And, of course, on occasion the hope was expressed that despite the failure of the European Defense Community (EDC), the increasing community between the Six might have useful consequences from the defense point of view. For instance, at the discussions at Haverford already referred to, Ben Moore raised the question whether it might not be possible to rescue from the EDC the idea of an arms pool in Europe, to get this put up as a European idea by some member of the Six, with the notion that the Americans would be willing to finance such an enterprise so as to provide a more economical and effective method of equipping the NATO forces.[2]

The fact that many Americans believed that the intervention of the United States had worked against the possible ratification of the EDC, made them careful to avoid the appearance of any undue interest when things in Europe began to go ahead again with the Messina Conference of May 1955. Jean Monnet himself had, indeed, been in touch with some of his American contacts in the previous six months, and on an unofficial basis there was a constant interchange of ideas. But the main argument was within Monnet's own circle, as between his original idea of an extension of the sector approach and the more

---

[1] Important works summarizing the state of the debate at the times at which they were written are *NATO and the Future of Europe*, edited by Ben T. Moore (Harper, 1958), *Alliance Policy in the Cold War*, edited by Arnold Wolfers (Johns Hopkins Press, 1959), and R. E. Osgood, *NATO, the Entangling Alliance* (University of Chicago Press, 1962).

[2] H. Field Haviland, Jr. (ed.), *The United States and the Western Community* (Haverford College Press, 1957), p. 149.

radical proposal that eventually prevailed of going direct for a full Common Market. Once the post-Messina negotiations got going, the United States (unlike the United Kingdom in this respect) firmly believed in the possibility of a successful outcome.

Many people, though perhaps not Monnet himself, believed that the proposal for a European Atomic Energy Community (EURATOM) was more important than that for a Common Market. In relation to EURATOM, United States policy was all-important. The Americans shared the general miscalculations prevalent at the time about the energy requirements of Europe and the future availability of non-atomic sources of energy. Even more important was the fact that they believed that the novelty of the atomic field made it a suitable one in which to create new institutions, since few vested interests existed to be disturbed. United States cooperation here was more necessary than in regard to tariff arrangements because of the fact that it controlled the requisite materials. It was also concerned with the proposed controls of the uses to which atomic energy might be put.

In the Haverford discussions in 1956, there was indeed some evidence that people considered EURATOM largely in relation to the desirability of preventing the proliferation of nuclear armaments in the NATO countries which might affect the solidarity of the alliance. Once again the question was raised whether the United States could make it a condition of assistance that a community of a supranational character be established.

A conference was held at Princeton University in May 1956 on the subject of "EURATOM and American Policy," and the rapporteur, Professor Klaus Knorr, made it clear that the general view had been that EURATOM was in the interests of the United States to the extent that it contributed to the economic strength of Western Europe. It was held that such a development would not be out of step with the creation of the international agency in this field that was being set up under the auspices of the United Nations. Although this group also reached the conclusion that American policy should be favorable to the proposed EURATOM, it was felt undesirable that this concern should be given any unduly dramatic expression.

A decisive step was perhaps that taken by President Eisenhower when he announced in February 1957 that the United States would allocate fuel for sale or lease outside the country, and there were also indications that the United States would look with favor on other requests for assistance to the proposed community, of either a financial or a technical kind. The EURATOM Treaty itself, signed on March 25, 1957, was ambiguous in some respects; it did not prevent, as France was to show, the member countries from going ahead in the armaments field. But its contribution to European integration made it basically satisfactory to the United States and enabled the necessary legislation for assistance to it to be carried through Congress. The treaty came into force on January 1, 1958, and in November of that year the community concluded an important agreement with the United States for the supply to it of nuclear reactor stations of United States design, to be owned and operated by existing public utilities within the member countries.

The treaty setting up the European Economic Community (EEC) (the Common Market) was negotiated simultaneously with the EURATOM Treaty and was signed on the same date. One important reason for the relatively rapid conclusion of such complicated treaties was the effect in Europe of the Suez crisis. Indeed, although the United States deliberately played a much less active role after Messina than during the Schuman Plan and the EDC periods, its own policies were bound to affect everything that went on in Europe. For Suez not only exhibited the weakness and vulnerability of the Western European countries, but also in the view of some European statesmen the readiness of the United States to sacrifice what it regarded as vital interests in pursuit of its own world-wide policies.

It was, of course, important that the United States from its own point of view should follow the course of the negotiations, and an important group of people both inside and outside the government were concerned to study the possible effects of the conclusion of such an agreement on the trading position of the United States. They could not, of course, foresee the acceleration of the program of tariff reductions between the countries of the Common Market, nor the fact that the United States would contemporaneously run into serious balance-of-payments difficulties. But they did not overlook the general importance of the issues. Awareness of this kind, however, was not widespread in the country as a whole and was not even present throughout the administration.

On one particular point the United States was not happy about the final agreement, mainly the provision for associated territories overseas. Indeed, such association, which discriminated against other suppliers of tropical products, was at first condemned by the Americans. However, the objections were apparently overruled because of the political importance attached to the success of the negotiations by the President and the State Department. It was, indeed, necessary that these provisions should be accepted if France were to accede to the treaty. It might be added that at a later date the United Kingdom persuaded the United States to raise the question once more. But it took a different form once Britain's application for membership in the Common Market came forward, and the original objections disappeared from view.

Within the United States, opinion again tended to divide according to calculations about the impact of all these developments on the American economy itself. There was worry in agricultural circles and consequently in the Department of Agriculture. On the other hand the Department of Labor, reflecting the attitude of the trade union movement, was by and large favorable.

The unfavorable developments in the American economy that coincided with the coming into force of the Rome Treaty in January 1958 brought about some reconsideration of the whole position with regard to European integration. Some professional economists still criticized the favor shown toward the integration movement, but such critics by now represented the view of only a small minority in American government circles.[3] More representative figures argued that since agricultural goods had never moved in accordance with the rules of the General Agreement on Tariffs and Trade (GATT), and since the United States, Great Britain, and the Common Market countries were responsible for 90 percent of the world's trade in industrial goods, there was no incompatibility between the regional approach to economic problems and the traditional American commitment to multilateralism. Furthermore, on the monetary side there was in the years after 1958 a movement toward multilateralism on the Bretton Woods model.

More relevant than the economic criticism was perhaps the fact that from 1958 onward the priority of Europe in American thinking

[3] For the critics' argument, see, for instance, Isaiah Frank, *The European Common Market: An Analysis of Commercial Policy* (Praeger, 1961).

was seriously called into question. Americans tended to be more concerned with the technological rivalry with the Soviet Union after the launching of the first Soviet space satellite. They were increasingly concerned with their position in the underdeveloped countries and the need to meet Soviet economic and political penetration in such areas. European policy was considered largely in relation to problems of this kind.

While the Americans had been in the background during the negotiations that led to the Rome treaties themselves, they were, of course, concerned with what might subsequently happen in world trade, and in particular with the reactions of the remaining countries of Western Europe. In 1956 the six countries that were to form the Common Market accepted as their working document the Spaak Report, which suggested that a free trade area covering the whole of Western Europe could be superimposed on the suggested customs union of the Six. In November 1956 the idea of a European Free Trade Area became official British policy. [4]

The British put this forward in some circles as a concession to the European point of view, although it was not generally so regarded in the Six. The proposals were held up so as not to interfere with the negotiations of the Rome Treaty itself, and negotiations did not begin until October 1957. They continued until their final breakdown in January 1959.[5]

It is not clear how far if at all United States policy was responsible for this breakdown. In official pronouncements in January 1957 and April 1957, both the plans of the Six for a Common Market and the Free Trade Area were welcomed on an equal footing provided that they showed a liberal attitude to the outside world, particularly in the case of agricultural products. At a meeting of the Maudling Committee, which was in charge of the Free Trade Area negotiations, on February 17, 1958, the American observer made a statement in which he pointed out that the United States government hoped the negotiations would be successful and warned the committee that a split between the European states would make the renewal of the Trade Agreements Act by Congress more difficult.

[4] U. W. Kitzinger, *The Challenge of the Common Market* (Oxford, 1961), pp. 86–87.

[5] For an account of these events from the British angle, see Max Beloff, *New Dimensions in Foreign Policy* (London, 1961), pp. 99–109.

In March 1958, the French produced counterproposals for a free trade area of a highly protectionist kind, which opened a critical stage in the negotiations. At the beginning of the following month the United States addressed itself to all member governments of the Organization for European Economic Corporation (OEEC), making its position clear. It stated that it would support the Free Trade Area only if it was compatible with the GATT and took the interests of third countries fully into account. The French proposals were unacceptable and would be opposed within the GATT. It was important that the negotiations on the Free Trade Area should not endanger the implementation of the Common Market Treaty because the Community of the Six provided the starting point for a genuine political integration. On the other hand, the United States government feared that a breakdown of the negotiations might react unfavorably both on the situation in Europe and on NATO. It was therefore prepared to support the proposals of the EEC commission for an interim solution, namely the extension to all members of the GATT of the first round of tariff reductions under the treaty.

Finally, at the crucial OEEC meeting of December 15, 1958, which heralded the final breakdown, several delegations asked the American observer to act as mediator, pointing out that this would be in line with the traditional American policy of supporting unification. The United States observer refused, however, to take any position on the dispute between the United Kingdom and France which was the issue at the time.

This record of the American interventions in the Free Trade Area negotiations may well be incomplete, but it is sufficient to suggest that the administration may have been divided internally about the desirability of the proposal and about its political implications in particular. Some of its members may well have been influenced by Monnet's original belief that Britain was in effect trying to weaken the cooperation of the Six among themselves. There is some suggestion that Dulles tried to sway the German Economics Minister Ludwig Erhard from his originally favorable attitude toward the British scheme.[6] Douglas Dillon, a powerful figure in the State Department, was hostile to the British idea, and the British Prime Minister's efforts

[6] Roscoe Drummond and Gaston Coblentz, *Dual at the Brink* (Doubleday, 1960), pp. 196–97.

to enlist President Eisenhower's support were unsuccessful. Some people argue that in 1957 it would still have been possible to persuade France to go along with the British plan, though this was admittedly no longer true after de Gaulle took office in 1958. From this point of view, it is arguable that the mere quiescence of the United States was quite enough to make the project fail. Others say that the United States attitude was beside the point altogether and that the reasons for the failure of the scheme must be sought wholly in Europe.

The American objections can certainly be understood. It was maintained that with European currency convertibility in sight, as was shown by the coming into force of the European Monetary Agreement, which replaced the European Payments Union in December 1958, the Europeans no longer required American economic support, and that there were therefore no economic arguments for having a special regional system. Regional economic arrangements in Europe were henceforward only to be accepted if they could be justified by political arguments, as in the case of the Community of the Six. The proposed Free Trade Area presented no such political attractions. More broadly, it has been suggested that the ultimate reason was "the suspicion on the part of some that the United Kingdom's primary purpose, in line with its historic continental policy, was to prevent the emergence of a single powerful entity on the Continent." [7] Still more simply, it was held that the United Kingdom quite clearly did not want the kind of Europe that appealed to the United States.

In 1959, after the failure of the Free Trade Area negotiations, the British went ahead with the creation of a Free Trade Association, comprising the United Kingdom, the Scandinavian countries, Switzerland, Austria, and Portugal, and the treaty setting it up was initialed on November 20. It was made very plain to the countries concerned that this grouping was not in the American view deserving of the approval that the activities of the Six elicited. Indeed, some overt hostility toward it was scarcely concealed. The reasons once again, are not far to seek: "It may be argued that the contrast between the strong and outspoken United States government support for the Common Market of the Six and the relatively noncommittal official American attitude

[7] Eric Stein and T. L. Nicholson (eds.), *American Enterprise in the European Common Market: A Legal Profile*, 2 vols. (University of Michigan Press, 1960), pp. 5–6.

toward the proposed Outer Seven Free Trade Area [i.e. association] project was explainable by the overriding political importance of the Common Market as a stage in the development of the political unity of the Six whereas the Free Trade Area was viewed as a purely commercial arrangement." [8]

In conformity with this general approach, the United States took a still more unfavorable attitude toward the British attempt to "build bridges," as it was called, between the two groups that had come into being in Europe. Americans had become unsympathetic to what was now the British view that the division of Europe into these two commercial groupings would have unfavorable political consequences. They also argued that the kind of proposals envisaged would not conform to the GATT. In fact, the United States government maintained little direct contact with Britain on these matters in the period between the breakdown of the EFTA discussions and the end of the Eisenhower Presidency. In the British view, this partly reflected a general slowing down of the drive in American foreign policy after the disappearance of Dulles. Americans attributed it to the feeling in Britain that the British would lack sympathy with their policy particularly on the part of Mr. Dillon, and to their hope for a different line from the new administration.[9] The revision in the British official attitude that took place presumably during 1960 and which led to the conclusion that the best solution would be for Britain to enter the Common Market provided that American approval and perhaps assistance could be obtained, was reached without direct consultation with the United States government. While certain contacts between Canada and the United States were maintained during this period, these did not cover the problem of what would happen to the Commonwealth preferences if the United Kingdom eventually followed this line of action.

It would be a mistake, of course, to regard the United States attitude as a wholly passive one during these years. According to one authority it was toward the end of 1959 that the United States government, professing its concern about the apparently growing dispute on commercial policy between the Six and the Seven, and worried about Amer-

[8] Frank, *op. cit.*, pp. 127–28.

[9] The contrast between American and British attitudes toward European developments was strikingly illustrated at the so-called "Atlantic Congress" which celebrated the first decade of NATO at a meeting in London in June 1959.

ica's own balance of payments, decided to abandon neutrality and intervene.[10] American intervention eventually led to the acceptance of an American proposal for reorganizing the OEEC into what became the Organization for Economic Cooperation and Development (OECD). This organization would include the United States and Canada, which would have responsibilities in the field of coordinating trade policies and also aid policy in the underdeveloped countries, where greater European participation might lessen the strain on the American balance of payments. But the original motive of the United States for favoring the recasting of OEEC was not worry over the balance of payments but a feeling that the marginal position of the United States was no longer appropriate. Congress was not given a full account of what the administration hoped to gain by the change.

It was still clear, however, that the United States was favorable to the Community of the Six, and particularly the acceleration of their progress toward a full Common Market, which was decided on in May 1960. At about the same time, the evidence of a new flexibility in the British approach became apparent, with the announcement in June of the British willingness to consider membership of the Coal and Steel Community and of EURATOM. The failure of the Paris summit meeting in May may have had something to do with the further development of British policy in the remainder of the year: "One step at a time but with surprising swiftness as both the Berlin and the sterling problem seemed to grow worse, the Government moved towards Europe." [11]

From the American point of view, the possibility of a merger between the Six and the Seven naturally raised new questions. It was pointed out that it would substantially add to the amount of diversion of United States goods, so that the question was whether there would be enough offsetting benefits to justify this fact: "If the merger involves full entry into the Common Market by the Seven, or at least by the U.K., the political benefit would appear to justify major economic sacrifices by the U.S." [12] The possibility that a wider form of Euro-

[10] Emile Benoit, *Europe at Sixes and Sevens: The Common Market* (Columbia University Press, 1961) p. 92.

[11] Kitzinger, *op. cit.*, p. 105.

[12] Benoit, *op. cit.*, p. 255. The same author added that while there would be this diversionary impact on U.S. exports to Europe, the production by European countries for their own enlarged markets might release other markets for U.S. exporters. They would benefit, too, if there were to be an increased rate of growth in the

pean integration might lead to a reemergence of "third force" ideas was taken into account, but generally speaking discounted. On the other hand, it was realized that on the commercial side the emergence of an industrial power on the scale of an enlarged Common Market might lead to a necessary reconsideration of the United States commercial policy and to questioning the utility in this connection of the bargaining procedures hitherto followed in the GATT.[13]

Even if one is correct in assuming, as some observers did at the time, that the creation of the OECD had more to do with the United States new interest in development programs than with its commercial balance, the growing concern about the latter and the very existence of the OECD were bound to raise anew the question, which had been in the minds of a number of Americans throughout the decade, of extending the European scale of operations to the whole Atlantic community. The reasons for this had always been as much political as economic. Indeed, many of those troubled primarily about security questions had been anxious that every advance in Europe should coincide with a further strengthening of the Atlantic Alliance.[14]

Some of the men who had been most active in promoting concern with Europe early took up the cause of Atlantic unity. For instance, William Clayton became one of the two vice-presidents of the Atlantic Union Committee in 1949 and made a number of speeches in support of some kind of Atlantic federation in the course of the next two or three years.[15] But as we have seen in relation to the so-called "Green Book" of 1952, such ideas appealed only to a minority in American official circles.

Among the important effects of the failure to keep progress on the Atlantic and on the European fronts in step was the encouragement it afforded to British opponents of going more deeply into Europe. Denis Healey, a prominent spokesman for the Labour opposition, told the meeting at Haverford in 1956 already referred to that the

---

European community—though this would not apply to agriculture unless the EEC countries were willing to divert labor to industry and to rely more on cheap food imports. The calculation was further complicated by direct U.S. investment in European industry which had been growing ever since 1952.

[13] *Ibid.*, pp. 256–59.

[14] Klaus Knorr, *Euratom and American Policy* (May 1956) , pp. 16–17.

[15] E. C. Garwood, *Will Clayton: A Short Biography* (University of Texas Press, 1958) , pp. 34–36.

main reason for the setback to the European movement in the last five years lay not in Paris, Bonn, or London but in Washington: "It is the failure of the Atlantic community to develop as this closer supranational community originally envisaged which has undermined the British association with the continent and the French association with Germany." [16]

Among his American interlocutors, considerable skepticism was expressed about the possibility of progress ever being made in this direction: "For any regional or functional arrangement involving the United States, the most casual glance at domestic political realities will show that any formal institutional pooling of sovereignty is out of the question, both now and for the foreseeable future." [17] And this remark by Lincoln Gordon was put into an even wider context by Raymond Vernon when he said of his own contribution to the discussion:

> You will notice, too, that I have given no consideration to the possibility that the United States might merge its sovereign economic powers in some organic way with the rest of the Atlantic community. This is simply not in the cards; it would be resisted with equal vehemence by the Senator from Nevada, the backbencher from Lancashire, and the deputy from Rouen. It is not a possibility except in a world so greatly altered from that we know as to be barely recognizable.[18]

When, in 1956, Senator Estes Kefauver reintroduced in the Senate his Atlantic Union proposals originally put forward, as we have seen, as long ago as July 1949, hearings were held. But they were broken off and further hearings postponed on the advice of Secretary Dulles, who said that they would cut across the work of the NATO Council which was itself exploring ways of achieving a greater unity.

The idea of an Atlantic community did not really become actual again until Britain's intention to apply for membership in the Common Market was announced in the British Prime Minister's speech of July 31, 1961. For at least one American former-diplomat there was a certain irony in the fact that this announcement had fallen to the lot

[16] "Britain's Attitude Towards European Integration," in H. Field Haviland, Jr., (ed.), *op. cit.*, p. 43.
[17] Lincoln Gordon, "Political Integration in the Free World Community," *ibid.*, p. 75.
[18] "Economic Aspects of the Atlantic Community," *ibid.*, p. 62.

of Harold Macmillan, for it was Macmillan himself who had told him as long ago as 1944 that Britain would maintain in the postwar world its historic attitude of aloofness from the affairs of continental Europe —a fact which had contributed to his surprise at the favorable attitude of Winston Churchill and Duncan Sandys in the early stages of the European movement.

The Department of State had, however, foreseen that the British might well come round to accepting the idea of entering the Common Market, and a number of technical studies of the problems that this would raise and of the technical implications of such a step had been completed before the end of 1960.

On the British side suspicions were understandably voiced whether the British government's change of attitude should not be explained in terms of direct American pressure. But although it could be argued that United States hostility to other forms of bridge-building between the Six and the Seven, which had been expressed once more early in 1961, made it more likely that Britain would end up by applying for entry into the Common Market, the argument cannot easily be pushed further. But it should perhaps be noticed that the decision was probably reached only after it was realized in London that President Kennedy's new administration was as committed to the success of the Six as its predecessors. The important positions entrusted in it to Douglas Dillon, to George Ball, who had acted as the legal agent for the European Economic Community in the United States and who was a long-standing close personal associate of Jean Monnet, and to Professor W. W. Rostow, were sufficient, though not the sole, indications of this fact.[19]

Other Americans who shared Monnet's original view that the creation of the Europe of the Six would eventually bring the British round to realizing that their own interests lay in joining this grouping may have followed him in treating Britain's immediate post-Messina policies as hostile to the Community, and then with him have accepted the reality of Britain's change of heart.

While indications of this change of heart had been given to Ball

[19] Professor W. W. Rostow's book, *The United States in the World Arena* (Harper, 1960) presents the case for a closely united Western Europe, including the United Kingdom, within the general context of United States world policy. It is interesting to compare this treatment of the subject with the arguments he had put forward in 1946.

in London in March, the decisive moment was reached when Macmillan visited the President at the beginning of April. The question was raised from the British, not the American side, and the American response was much affected by the fact that the British had already made up their minds. What Macmillan asked the President was, it appears, whether Britain's entry into the Common Market would threaten its "special relationship" with the United States. Assurances on this point were deemed sufficient to enable the United Kingdom to proceed with its application. The statement by Uwe Kitzinger that "President Kennedy just did not understand what special relationship Mr. Macmillan meant" [20] can scarcely be taken at its face value. Even though the British had no doubt attached more importance to their postwar links with the United States than vice versa, the mere involvement of the two countries in so many issues of world politics—the fact that the United Kingdom was, for instance, the only other Western power with nuclear armaments of its own—could not but multiply the contacts between the two governments, and make for that intimacy on the day-to-day level which was so resented, for instance, by General de Gaulle. Americans might not unreasonably have objected to British exaggerations of the importance of this factor, but hardly to the point of denying its significance altogether.

It was precisely in terms of the common political interests of the two countries that Britain's entry into Europe was discussed between the President and the Prime Minister. The United States government was concerned to emphasize that it looked to the United Kingdom to provide an element of stability in European politics, especially in the difficult period which it was thought would follow the passing from the scene of Chancellor Adenauer and General de Gaulle, and Mr. Macmillan made it clear that he agreed to the overriding importance of the political objectives. It was also felt in Washington that on the great issues of East-West relations, disarmament, and attitudes to the developing countries, the British position might prove nearer to that of the United States than the positions of Western Germany or France, and that Britain's voice would consequently tend to urge the European Community as a whole along lines satisfactory to the United States. Britain might also help to check any tendencies in the Six to become too protectionist and inward. Finally, with Britain in the Community,

[20] Kitzinger, op. cit., p. 144.

the preeminent significance of the Atlantic alliance was unlikely to be overlooked, and the United States could proceed in its endeavors to construct an "Atlantic Community." The only uneasiness on the American side was about the timing, whether it was not too early; but this uneasiness was not expressed lest it cast doubt on the United States appreciation of the historic nature of Britain's decision.

Americans did not, generally speaking, share the fears that some people in Britain and some Canadians, for instance, were to express after the British application became public: namely, that the United Kingdom might be forced to purchase the concessions it would require on the economic side before entry into the Common Market by political concessions to the more rigid views on East-West relations of Western Germany and France.

On the economic side, there was probably from the beginning some differences of interpretation that were to have an important effect when the detailed negotiations between the United Kingdom and the Six began. The United States government maintained the view, already discussed, that the enlargement of the Common Market involved discrimination against America's own economic interests which only substantial political gains could justify. Outside the United States, however, some different points of view were stressed. Some Canadians and Australians, for instance, believed that the United States might emerge as the principal commercial beneficiary of these developments. For there would then be no preferences within the United Kingdom for Commonwealth products as against American products, while in the Commonwealth countries themselves the preferences British goods enjoyed over American goods would also be swept away.

CHAPTER IX

The United States and the Europe of the Six

BY THE SUMMER OF 1961 there was in the relevant sectors of the United States administration a fairly clear doctrine regarding the American position on the question of European unity. The doubts of the multilateralist economists had been put aside, and there was a strong commitment to the view that the creation of a United States of Europe should take precedence over all other considerations. It was hoped that the Treaty of Rome would provide the basis for an ever-increasing degree of economic integration, which in itself should contribute both to the freeing of world trade and to the ability of the European countries to assist the United States in the task of overseas development. It was held that such an economic union could be endowed with a political superstructure sufficiently powerful to enable the European countries to play a full part in devising and prosecuting policies of resistance to the Communist threat. Finally, it was held that the European communities should be expanded to include Britain and the two Scandinavian members of NATO. But there was some difference of opinion on what should be done about the remaining countries of Europe outside the Soviet bloc. Some people would have wished to expand the power of the Organization for Economic Co-operation and Development (OECD), others to find forms of association between such countries and the Communities, while yet others felt that no particular arrangements need be made.

The importance of the fact that the American government now had the guide-lines for action should not lead one to lose sight of the fact that the pace of development was still being set by what was going on in Europe itself.

Since August 1961 the main problems before Europe have been those posed by the application of the United Kingdom to join the Common Market, the probable effect of this application on the remaining members of EFTA, only some of which were in a position to follow the British example, and that of the likely effect on the Common Market of the entry into it of a country such as Britain, with its world-wide political, commercial, and financial commitments, together with the possible assistance that membership might give to Britain in meeting the difficulties created by these commitments, particularly in relation to the crucial questions of the balance of payments and of reserves.[1] Clearly, the even progress of the Common Market could not but be effected by a change in membership of this importance, and Monnet himself, while satisfied regarding the economic advantages of the proposed new development, was reported to be uncertain concerning the political forms that Western Europe might now find appropriate, and even to be wondering whether the political problem would not need to be transcended by a revival of the Atlantic community idea.

In fact, of course, it was not only the prospect of the British entry that called into question the core of the Monnet doctrine of 1950—an evolution toward ever tighter forms of political union through the compulsive effect of progressive economic integration. The coming into power in France of General de Gaulle had produced a new emphasis in French policy on national sovereignty, a rejection of many of the current assumptions about the interdependence of the countries of the Western Alliance, and a claim for parity in its direction with the English-speaking countries. The effect of this change on NATO falls outside the scope of this study. But in Europe the French plan for political union—the idea of "l'Europe des patries"—ran in a contrary direction to the federalist trends of the preceding period, and was even thought by some people to threaten the existing achievements of the economic community. A still further complication was inherent in the fact that while the French proposal seemed to be closer to the kind of political union that the British might find most acceptable, General de Gaulle himself, concerned above all to sustain the integrity of the

[1] For a recent discussion of the economic aspects of the Common Market from an American point of view rather skeptical about the value of "regional trading blocs," see Don D. Humphrey, *The United States and the Common Market* (Praeger, 1962).

Paris-Bonn axis and clearly suspicious of Britain, was averse to bringing the British into the political talks, and by no means enthusiastic,
it appeared, about bringing the British into Europe at all.

One could thus note by the spring of 1962 the curious paradox that
the demands for British participation in negotiations for further steps
toward political union in Europe came from precisely those countries
—Holland and Belgium—which were most devoted to the full federalist doctrine that Britain was least likely to accept.

The United States, although much concerned both with the British
negotiations for admission to the Common Market and with the intermittent discussions among the countries of the Six on the future political organization of a United Europe, was itself still not a partner in
the talks. But because of the importance of the United States in the
general context of world economic policy and of Western defense, its
views could not but be influential. It may well be that the extent of
this influence was not universally appreciated in the United States.
Indeed, many Americans seem to have come to the view that Britain's
application for entry into the Common Market was synonymous with
the completion of the process for its admission. It could almost be said
that the propaganda in the United States by the European Community and its American backers had been too successful in that many
Americans now believed that the federalist solution in Europe had
finally won the day and that the United Kingdom was simply going to
sign on the dotted line both the Rome Treaty and a political treaty
which the Six might soon conclude.

The United States was, of course, likely to be affected directly by the
impact on the world economy of the addition to the existing European
Economic Community (EEC) of so important a country as Britain,
and had to consider in detail the likely result of this expansion of the
Community from the point of view of the world economy as a whole.
It was favorable in principle to this development because it saw in it
not only political advantages absent from Britain's former Free
Trade Area proposals but also the possibility of using Britain's entry
as a means of harmonizing United States policies in Europe with the
original aspirations of the United States for a greater measure of
freedom in world trade generally.

The United States had to take into account the more direct question of the interests of its producers, particularly of agricultural commodities, when considering the suggestions made by Britain for variations in the treaty arrangements to suit the needs of its own economy and of Commonwealth producers.

In this respect, there was some danger lest the United States, instead of facilitating agreement between Great Britain and the Six, might make such agreement more difficult. It was made clear by the British government that the entry of Britain into the Common Market could only be made acceptable to the British Parliament and people if suitable long-term arrangements were made for easing the shock to Commonwealth producers. The Americans, despite their frequent use of congressional opposition as a reason for their inability to do particular things of importance to foreign governments, did not appear to be much concerned about the internal political problems that were bound to confront a British government suggesting changes of this magnitude, and that would be made even greater by any suggestion that the interests of Commonwealth countries were being betrayed. The Americans were unwilling to consider any far-reaching association for major Commonwealth countries that might mean a dilution of the political aspect of the European Community, and any but the most limited and temporary concessions in respect of the common tariff.

The American attitude on temperate zone foodstuffs was, of course, influenced by the fact that Western Europe had traditionally been the largest purchaser of American farm products. But in regard to tropical products there was also the difficulty that preferential treatment for the former British territories in Africa, similar to that allowed to the colonial and former colonial territories of the Six in the Treaty of Rome itself, might mean discrimination against the Latin American countries, which were increasingly at the center of American interest in the underdeveloped world. The American position on the latter point would seem to have been toned down in the course of the negotiations, since the Six were able to propose or envisage fairly generous treatment for Britain's former tropical possessions in a way that would have been thought unlikely had American objections persisted.

Where the Americans aligned themselves with the Europeans was in their opposition generally speaking to the prolongation indefinitely of Commonwealth preferences and to their extension from the United Kingdom market itself to the enlarged Common Market.

Some Americans were fully appreciative of the importance of the Commonwealth countries to the world economy and to political stability, and believed that it was possible to find alternative arrangements that would allow Britain to enter Europe without damage to Commonwealth interests. Some diplomacy was deployed by Washington, notably in the case of Australia, to convince Commonwealth statesmen of the soundness of this position. In so far as the industrial products, particularly of the Asian Commonwealth countries, were concerned, the United States was also in favor of attempting to deal with these problems by world-wide arrangements rather than on a basis of preferential treatment for Commonwealth countries in particular. Here they were obviously concerned with the interests of countries in Asia outside the Commonwealth, and particularly in some respects with those of Japan.

While these economic arguments were not unacceptable to the British government, and while sentiment in Britain was more and more accepting the view that the main purpose of the modern Commonwealth was to serve as a bridge between white and colored peoples and between developed and underdeveloped areas, this was not the way in which the position presented itself to important sectors of British public opinion. It was a dangerous thing to underestimate the pull which the old Commonwealth countries of predominantly European stock—Canada, Australia, and New Zealand—might still exercise on the United Kingdom electorate. In this respect, some of the continental European countries seemed to exhibit a livelier and deeper appreciation than many Americans did of the full significance of the step that Britain was being asked to take.

Some of the continental countries also, notably Western Germany with its strong commercial link with Austria, Sweden, and Switzerland, were closer to the British position than to the American one on the vexed question of the role of the European neutrals. American unwillingness to see the neutrals brought inside the Common Market had been made clear even before the British application. There is some reason to believe that in May 1961 a suggestion was made that EFTA should simply be abandoned with the NATO members coming in to the EEC and the neutrals staying outside. In any event, Britain entered on the negotiations for its entry into the Common Market with an explicit and formal commitment to seeking acceptable terms for its EFTA partners.

It was true that it was very difficult to give detailed attention to the exceptional position of these three countries, Sweden, Switzerland, and Austria, while the question of Britain's entry itself was still under debate. But the possibility of a formula for their association had to be at least considered if Britain was to bring the negotiations to a successful conclusion without breaking its pledges to the EFTA countries in such a way as to weaken it both internationally and electorally. Nevertheless, although there was some recognition of the peculiar position of Austria because of its treaty commitments, there seemed to be an element of rigidity in the American opposition to giving any of these countries some form of associated status. These objections could not be argued seriously on grounds of economic advantage. The three countries, which accounted for only 3 percent of United States trade, could not by having a preferential position in the Common Market vitally weaken America's opportunities there. Indeed, the argument was from the beginning essentially a political one. Association with the Common Market would confer economic advantages on these countries which they ought, so it was felt, to pay for by accepting the burdens of political and military cooperation, that is, by assuming the full implications of what Americans regarded as the principal purpose of the Economic Community, namely political union. That is to say that in the American view these countries could not accept the institutional requirements and voting procedures of the communities.

The argument that in their different ways both Swedish and Swiss neutrality could be a positive benefit to Western Europe was not accepted, and it seemed to many continental Europeans, as well as to the British, as if in these discussions the ghost of John Foster Dulles, with his deep conviction of the immorality of any form of neutrality in the East-West conflict, had made quite an inappropriate reappearance on the stage. Nor, I think, would the British government have been much moved by the argument that if no arrangements were found for the neutrals, it might be convenient to have the United States as a scapegoat if Britain were accused of letting them down. What moved the United States government to give so much emphasis to its views on this point was the conviction that unless Britain were prepared to negotiate alone and not in a body with or simultaneously with the other EFTA countries, the Six would not be ready to negotiate at all.

The discussion about European matters in the United States in the first year and a half of President Kennedy's administration was then largely directed toward considering the likely impact of the expansion of the European Economic Community on the United States itself. It is in this light that one must account for the most striking feature of the discussion, namely the revival of interest in the idea of an Atlantic Community. The idea of extending European cooperation into some kind of union on an Atlantic scale was mooted not only by enthusiasts of long standing, such as Senator Fulbright, but also by men who had hitherto been rather chary of committing themselves to far reaching notions of this kind, such as Dean Acheson and Lincoln Gordon.

In a speech to the Commonwealth Parliamentary Conference in London on September 30, 1961, Senator Fulbright said: "Britain's entry into the European Economic Community will not only contribute to the economic growth and welfare of Britain and Europe; it will mark a significant step towards the evolution of a genuine community of the North Atlantic—a community that must of necessity include the United States, and perhaps as well a step towards the emergence of a broader concert of free nations." His views were expanded in an article in the October issue of *Foreign Affairs*.

In a speech by John McCloy on November 29, reference was made to the desirability of joining in due course:

> . . . this composite of Great Britain and Europe . . . With the resources and strength of the United States and the Americas. . . . I do insist [he went on], that we must seek new and better forms wherein our common economic and political interests can be weighed, determined and acted upon. . . . We may have to set up some political institutions in which these great problems, which for a long time have been fully identified, can be dealt with and a common policy worked out in regard to them.

Some people, indeed, felt that the matter was urgent. A press release on December 27, 1961, from the "National Committee for an Effective Congress" ran in part:

Today this simple truth is becoming apparent to Washington as well as to Wall Street: that a Europe organized without the United States would be a Europe organized against the United States. This is why we are pushing hard for Britain joining the Common Market without delay. We need Britain as a broker and to ensure an open door. For if we fail to strengthen our political ties with NATO and don't establish a free world Common Market, we may see the economic community of continental Europe and Africa, become a separate political bloc, which could be a third great power, equal in strength to Russia and the United States, and uncommitted between the two. The emergence of such a fortress Europe would crack the historic unity of Western civilization, upon which rest the hopes of free men and free institutions.

The climax of this phase of the discussion came with the address by Secretary of State Rusk to the annual meeting of the American Historical Association on December 30, when he talked of "a wholesome ferment in Europe and throughout the Atlantic community generating a debate which historians may well rank with the great constitutional debate of the 1780's." He then went on to picture American policy since the war as one of a "grand design" leading from the original commitment to assist in uniting Europe to a "pattern of constructive association among the whole of the northern half of the world, from Tokyo to Bonn, and with the new nations to the south."

But there was a persistent ambiguity regarding the political significance of such declarations, because in terms of policy what seemed to be envisaged was a purely economic response to the challenge—a more liberal trading policy based on the old principles of multilateralism and nondiscrimination.[2]

It was clear that supporters of this drive for a new commerical policy did not necessarily envisage political consequences. Indeed, it was hard to see how anything of the kind was conceivable once the geographical framework of the North Atlantic Alliance was bypassed. Even George Ball himself, the great protagonist of supranationalism for Europe, while declaring in a much quoted speech on November 1, 1961, that the political strengthening of the free world could be brought about through the added economic strength of a

[2] See the powerful arguments for such a policy in two papers presented in December to the U.S. Joint Economic Committee: Robert R. Bowie and Theodore Geiger, *The European Economic Community and the United States*, and Henry S. Reuss, *The Tasks for 1962: A Free World Community*, 87 Cong., 1 sess.

wider trading system, did not suggest any institutional underpinning. And Christian Herter joined with William Clayton in a public statement that talked merely of the United States forming "a trade partnership with the European Economic Community" and taking "the leadership in further expanding a free world economic community." [3]

What is remarkable about Herter's position is that he was one of the principal movers in the Atlantic Convention of NATO Nations which took place in Paris from January 8 to January 20, 1962, and in which the participants, although private citizens, were appointed by their governments, in the case of the United States under an act of Congress which Herter's influence had helped to secure. Among other resolutions, one of those accepted by the convention was as follows: "The delegates" call upon the governments of the NATO countries to draw up plans within two years for the creation of an Atlantic community suitably organized to meet the political, military, and economic challenges of this era. To this end they should, within the earliest practicable period, "appoint members to a special governmental commission on Atlantic unity. The commission should study the organization of the Atlantic community, particularly in the light of the recommendations at this Convention, and it should be instructed to propose such reforms and simplifications of existing institutions, and such new institutions as may be required."

A warning not to take too seriously all that was being said about Atlantic union came from the highest level of all. In his speech to the National Association of Manufacturers on December 6 President Kennedy said : "I am not proposing, nor is it desirable, that we join the Common Market, alter our concepts of political sovereignty, establish a 'rich man's' trading community, abandon our traditional most-favored-nation policy, create an Atlantic free trade area, or impair in any way our close economic ties with Canada, Japan, or the rest of the free world." And in a speech on the same day, McGeorge Bundy, one of the President's closest advisers in this field, while again stressing the importance of responding to the Common Market in terms of "a grand design for prosperous and expanding trade in the free world," specifically repudiated a "full-blown Atlantic union" in favor

---

[3] *A New Look at Foreign Economic Policy in the Light of the Cold War and the Extension of the Common Market in Europe*, a paper presented to the U.S. Joint Economic Committee, 87 Cong., 1 sess.

of a "partnership between the United States on the one hand and a great European power on the other."

The proposals made by President Kennedy for a new trade expansion act in his message to Congress of January 25, 1962, were on the lines he had foreshadowed.[4] While the authority he sought for tariff bargaining would be used primarily to secure reductions in the common tariff of the EEC, all other non-Communist countries of the world would benefit equally through the application of the most-favored-nation principle. Nor were any special institutional devices envisaged.

Although the arguments for the new policy were largely expressed in terms of American self-interest, although flavored for domestic political reasons with a pronounced "cold war" element, it might have been asked what the success of such a policy would hold in store for the Common Market itself. For if the common tariff was to be a major instrument of economic integration between its members, what would happen if, as enthusiastic free traders hoped, tariffs fell into the same general desuetude as quotas. In a world of near zero tariffs, what magic would a common tariff possess? Some consideration had to be given to other ways in which the Common Market group might be held together.

It looks, indeed, as though the United States was in relation to Europe now more concerned with defense than with opulence, and that in so far as it was concerned with opulence, it was mainly with the idea of seeing that Europe's surplus was effectively channeled into aid to those other parts of the world where the major economic and ideological struggle against Communism was now being waged.

It was characteristic of this period that individuals in the administration began to show increasing concern to link up the existing policy of support for the Common Market with a broader approach to American foreign policy at large. In other words, a philosophy began to develop within which there would be room for a further step toward general free trade, as in the GATT agreement reached in

---

[4] The first proposal directed toward negotiating lower tariffs between the EEC and the United States had been put forward by Dillon at the GATT session in the fall of 1958. Congress had extended the Trade Agreements Act for four years instead of the usual three so as to give the U.S. greater bargaining power. see Frank, *op. cit.*, p. 183. The new act passed through Congress substantially unchanged and was signed by the President on October 11, 1962.

June 1962, for the Common Market, and for some kind of Atlantic partnership not only in trade but also in development and in defense. The book by Joseph Kraft, *The Grand Design*, subtitled significantly "From Common Market to Atlantic Partnership," may be taken as evidence of the kind of language talked in official circles in Washington in the summer of 1962. It also gives a good deal of information about the personalities involved in the creation and dissemination of these policies.[5] Another instrument for understanding the relationship between the European policy and these broader aims was provided by Professor W. W. Rostow, the Chairman of the Policy Planning Council of the State Department, in a lecture given by him at Purdue University on March 15, 1962.

Professor Rostow suggested that American strategy in the world at large should be thought of in five dimensions. First, "strengthening the bonds of association among the more industrialized nations, which lie mainly in the northern portion of the free world: Western Europe, Canada, and Japan"; second, the support of "the revolution of modernization going forward in Latin America, Africa, Asia, and the Middle East"; third, the building up of new ties between the northern and southern halves of the world, as for instance in the Alliance for Progress, in relations with the new African nations and in the Development Assistance Committee of the OECD; fourth, the military dimension—"we must protect what we are building or there will be no freedom"—and fifth, a complex attitude toward the Communist world, neither initiating nuclear war to destroy it nor accepting its existence in perpetuity. It is clear that an analysis of this kind assumes that success in the first four dimensions will contribute to a historical development within the Communist world which will eventually promote the creation of a single world community.

If in the light of such broad assessments of the situation one tries to place the particular problems presented by the emergence of the European Economic Community, one can see that American policy was bound increasingly to be influenced by non-European considerations. By the spring of 1962, then, it might be said that the United States objective in economic policy was to bring the whole of the non-Soviet world under the same regime of generally freer trade and payments, but within this world it saw an emergent grouping of two

[5] Joseph Kraft, *The Grand Design* (Harper, 1962) .

major centers of power—the United States and an integrated Western Europe including Britain. It was to this power relationship that Bundy's phrase the "Atlantic partnership" referred, and it was "Atlantic partnership" rather than "Atlantic union" that now seemed best to express the administration's objectives.

In this respect two speeches made by George Ball, at Philadelphia and Cincinnati on February 8 and February 19 deserve consideration. In the course of the first of these two addresses, which was entitled "Towards an Atlantic Partnership," Ball said that many would ask why America and Europe had not gone faster and further in forging an Atlantic partnership. To this he answered:

> A strong partnership must almost by definition mean a collaboration of equals. When one partner possesses over 50 percent of the resources of a firm, and the balance is distributed among sixteen or seventeen others, the relationship is unlikely to work very well. And so long as Europe remained fragmented, so long as it consisted merely of nations small by modern standards, the potentials for true partnership were always limited. It was in recognition of this fact [he went on] that since the war we have consistently encouraged the powerful drive toward European integration. We have wanted a Europe united and strong that could serve as an equal partner in the achievement of our common endeavors—an equal partner committed to the same basic values and objectives as all Americans.

All of these North Atlantic countries were dedicated not only to defending the free world, but to assisting the less fortunate nations to attain the strength that would give them self-respect and independence. It was this theme which was to be the burden of his second address, entitled "The Less Developed Countries and the Atlantic Partnership," and here he called attention to the OECD, in which were being perfected "techniques of consultation not only in monetary matters but in a whole range of fiscal and other domestic policies," since the OECD was "the first truly Atlantic organization in the economic field," just as NATO "was the Atlantic organization in the field of defense." Mr. Ball became increasingly the spokesman for the views of the government not only in the United States but also abroad. An address to the German Society for Foreign Affairs given at Bonn on April 2, 1962, entitled "The Developing Atlantic Partnership," set out for his audience the program by which the United States sought to reconcile itself to the "substantial degree of discrimination against

American trade" inherent in the Common Market by acting on two convictions: "first, that the Community would be conducted as an outward-looking society, liberal in its trading and economic policies, and second, that it would be increasingly prepared to bear responsibilities around the world as its strength and unity developed."

While the exposition of the detailed applications of thinking of this kind could be left to officials, the only way in which the ideas themselves could be made part of the general American thinking on world affairs was through their reiteration by the President himself. His contribution was forthcoming in the speech which he delivered at Philadelphia on July 4: "But I will say, here and now, on this Day of Independence, that the United States will be ready for a Declaration of Interdependence—that we will be prepared to discuss with a united Europe the ways and means of forming a concrete Atlantic partnership—a mutually beneficial partnership between the new union now emerging in Europe and the old American Union founded here a century and three quarters ago."

Enough has been said to indicate the economic thinking behind the discussion of the idea of an Atlantic partnership. For those who believed that the Community, particularly if Britain became a member, would fulfill their hopes of being outward-looking and of cooperating fully in the tasks of development in the poorer southern half of the world, the remaining problems were those of application rather than of principle. Where much less clarity was forthcoming in the summer of 1962 was on the military side. Here again, the need for rethinking American policy arose largely out of developments in Europe itself, notably the French insistence on independent nuclear strength and the likelihood that other countries, including the Federal Republic of Germany, would follow this example. Some people felt that in the long run such demands could not be resisted and that the best thing to do was to shape American policy in such a way as to turn this to positive ends. In other words, they argued that while individual national "deterrents" were dangerous, a united Europe including Britain could be allowed to become a nuclear power provided that it was closely aligned with the United States. The partnership between the two great economic areas of the northern half of the non-Communist world would thus be duplicated by a military partnership. This prospect was thought to offer two further advantages. In the first place, it might help to relieve the American balance-of-payments problem by promoting a partial running-down of the American military establishment in Europe.[6] In the second place, and this was more ominous for Europeans, it might allow for a large-scale American withdrawal if for one reason or another there was a growth in neo-isolationist sentiment.

From the practical point of view, it is obvious that such a line of thought made the Americans all the keener to see Britain enter the European Community, since it was believed that in working out the policies of such a partnership, the British would normally be closer to the American point of view than France or even Western Germany.

On the other side, the dominant doctrine still emphasized the undesirability for military reasons of any dispersal in the control of nuclear weapons, and sought a solution to the doubts about the Atlantic alliance in a greater degree of integration. This doctrine was behind the much discussed speech made by Secretary of Defense McNamara at the University of Michigan on June 16, 1962. While his references to nuclear power were semiofficially commented on as being directed against the development of independent deterrents on the European continent, it is clear that the logic of the case would equally apply to any further independent development of nuclear striking-power by Britain, its existing strength in this area being acceptable because of its almost complete integration with the American forces. Supporters of the McNamara doctrine denied the view lying behind the alternative approach, that a serious independent nuclear capability was within reach of the European countries, pointing out the immense disparity in the expenditure on defense that European countries had shown themselves willing to accept as compared with the United States. If, on the other hand, they insisted on having nuclear weapons of their own and were willing to pay for them, it was recognized in the American administration that this demand could not be resisted indefinitely. But in that case the American weight would certainly be thrown in favor of a multilateral force as against "national" deterrents. But they hoped that this political pressure might relax, that people would recognize the danger of encouraging the

[6] It may be noted in passing that just as the balance-of-payments problem had come on the United States very suddenly, so it was believed in some quarters that it might prove to be only a temporary phenomenon.

United States to contemplate withdrawal from Europe, and they argued that if some form of arms control agreement with the Communist world were ever to be achieved, this would be much less difficult if a single authority were in a position to negotiate for the whole of the Western world. Meanwhile, the administration continued to urge that the Europeans should increase their contribution to the common defense by raising additional conventional forces, and to discuss the possibility of adding to the United States deterrent, a "NATO" deterrent in the control of which the United States itself would participate.

Although the military situation gave rise to the most complex of the problems facing the countries of the Atlantic alliance in 1962, it seemed possible to some people that a further advance toward the creation of common institutions, might, as in the case of Western Europe, result from economic pressures. Such a feeling was not confined to the United States. In an article in October 1962, Lord Franks, a former British ambassador in Washington, pointed out that there were "four international economic problems of vital importance to the Atlantic group of nations . . . aid to developing countries, trade with developing countries, the means of international settlement and the surpluses of the temperate-zone agricultural products." But it was a false abstraction to describe them simply as economic problems: "They are political too, and, unless their political importance is grasped and understood, the will to deal with them will lack strength." After considering the developments in Europe in the past decade, Lord Franks continued: "If the Atlantic group of nations seriously wills the attainment of its broad political ends in the world and searches for common solutions to its economic problems on the international scale . . . it is difficult to see how this can be done except by adopting political procedures akin in some respects to those operating in the Six." [7] What he was suggesting was not the expansion of the Common Market to embrace the entire Atlantic community, but rather as a minimum a new Atlantic institution akin to the Common Market Commission, that is to say a group independent of any of the governments which would be in a position to formulate and advocate proposals to deal with their common problems. If such an institution

[7] Lord Franks, "Cooperation Is Not Enough," *Foreign Affairs* (October 1962), pp. 26, 27, 33.

were created, the governments would, so Lord Franks argued, face not merely each other's arguments but also, and at the same time, the "solution proposed for the partnership as a whole as best realizing its common good."

Since an institution of the kind envisaged by Lord Franks would not involve a formal surrender of decision-making powers such as the Common Market countries themselves had made, one might argue that the reaction of Americans to proposals of this kind would be a test of the extent to which they were genuinely willing to translate the new talk of an Atlantic partnership into concrete terms. Whether the reaction would be favorable or unfavorable, and whether indeed there existed in the United States in 1962 a sufficient body of support for any progress in this direction, was at least doubtful. It would seem to be the conclusion to be drawn from the fifteen years of history since the announcement of the Marshall Plan that the arguments about Atlantic unity tended to be circular ones. It was intellectually realized that many of the most important problems could not be resolved except on an Atlantic scale, but it was also felt that public opinion in the United States was so wary of any direct challenge to national sovereignty that only intergovernmental solutions were possible. On the other hand, where sentiment for national sovereignty and self-sufficiency was weaker, as in Western Europe, full advantage should be taken of the fact, and institutional expression be given to the acknowledged area of interdependence. But when this was done, the consequence was to raise anew problems of relevance to the whole Atlantic community and so to pose yet again the issue of its own institutions.

Despite the impressive quality of some of the statements made about interdependence and the Atlantic partnership in the first half of 1962, there was little evidence that they had great repercussions either in Congress or on opinion generally. The initial drive must largely have been exhausted by the efforts to carry through the new Trade Agreements policy, and when Congress finally adjourned, and the electoral campaign was joined, the issues placed before the voters had little relevance to the broad strategy of the "grand design."

It is not simply the general feeling in the United States that the country could and should make its own decisions in economic as in military matters, but also the tenacity of the United States governmental patterns of action that seem most relevant to this argument. It is difficult to see how a body such as Lord Franks suggests could be created without incurring a suspicion on the part of Congress that important decisions were going to be made by persons who would not be subject to the ordinary procedures of congressional control. In this sense the objections that were being put up in Britain in 1962 to membership of the Common Market, in particular the fear of an anonymous bureaucracy controlling the country's economic destinies, were all too likely to reappear on the American scene. It seemed doubtful that a Congress which was still so jealous of any extension of executive authority in the country's internal affairs would be more open to the idea that authority, even if only moral authority, should be transferred to an international body. It could be argued that the American attitude to the United Nations was significant in this respect. Where the United Nations was operating in fields remote from direct American interest, or where as in the Congo it could be used to help in the exclusion of Communist influences from an area considered important, the United States was prepared to go a long way in its support, even at times at the expense of agreement with its allies in Europe. The affairs of the Congo in 1961 seemed at moments to be reproducing almost the tensions that "Suez" had been responsible for within the alliance. But where it was a matter of the vital interests of the United States, the popular pressure to act directly rather than risk the powers of delay and obstruction inherent in the United Nations procedures was very strong.

The United States by 1962 was clearly a long way from the unsophisticated isolationism of 1920 or even from the more sophisticated hopes of 1944. But the obsolescence of national sovereignty that was the key to the process going on in Europe was something with which the American people had still to be confronted. For this reason it seemed more probable that relations between the United States and a united Western Europe would take a traditionally bilateral form rather than that they would lend themselves in the immediate future to any important institutional innovations. At any rate, there would seem to be insufficient grounds for thinking that the unity of Europe itself was already so well-established that it could be regarded as a problem of the past rather than of the future. It looks as though the

United States will still have to concern itself with the further working out of this process and that to end this narrative in the summer of 1962 is not to be taken as an indication that the process has reached its natural climax.

Much had been achieved in Western Europe over the years under consideration—remarkable economic growth, a surprising degree of reconciliation between countries deeply divided by recent wrongs, and a growing habit of consultation. But many of the issues that had faced American policy makers since the end of World War II were still present. What was to be the membership in the end of a United Europe? Was there any solution to the tension in Western Germany between national reunification and the subordination of this aspiration to increasing integration with Germany's western neighbors? Could Great Britain reconcile its European aims with its Commonwealth ties, and must a Western Europe looking outward across the ocean simultaneously turn its back on the remainder of the continent? Would the friendly concern of the Americans help in the solution of problems of this kind, and would this demand from them a high degree of political inventiveness as well as of the open-handedness that had by and large characterized their relations with Europe in the postwar world?

Index

124